D1714624

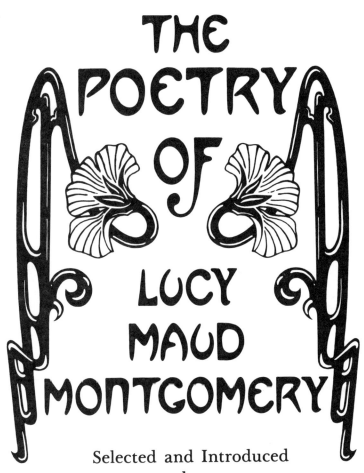

THE POETRY OF LUCY MAUD MONTGOMERY

Selected and Introduced
by
John Ferns and Kevin McCabe

Fitzhenry & Whiteside

To Gill and Sue

Fitzhenry & Whiteside
195 Allstate Parkway
Markham, Ontario L3R 4T8

Typeset by Jay Tee Graphics Ltd.
Printed and bound in Canada by
John Deyell Company

Canadian Cataloguing in Publication Data

Montgomery, L. M. (Lucy Maud), 1874-1942
  The poetry of Lucy Maud Montgomery
ISBN 0-88902-931-8
I. McCabe, Kevin, 1949- . II. Ferns, John,
1941- . III. Title.
PS8526.045A6 1987   C811'.52   C87-094541-6
PR9199.2.M6A6 1987

Contents

Acknowledgements

First, my thanks to Mary Rubio and Elizabeth Waterston of the University of Guelph for inviting me to undertake this project. Next, I thank Kevin McCabe for assisting me with it throughout. We both thank Rea Wilmshurst of the University of Toronto for supplying us with copies she had made of about five hundred poems by L.M. Montgomery that she had discovered in magazines, newspapers and in manuscript books of L. M. Montgomery's in Prince Edward Island during the course of her research on L. M. Montgomery's short fiction. Without this fundamental help the present selection would have been impossible.

Our thanks go to Mollie Gillen, Helen Heller and Robert Fitzhenry, acting for Fitzhenry & Whiteside, for their interest in and advice on the project. Mollie Gillen, in particular, deserves our thanks for advice about selections and presentation. We, of course, accept full responsibility for the selection and introduction. Marian Hebb for the L. M. Montgomery Estate deserves our thanks for arranging permission with Mrs. Ruth Macdonald to use published and unpublished material. Also, we thank Dean Askin and Wayne Collins of CBC, Charlottetown, for introducing our work on their morning radio programme.

Finally, we thank Gill and Sue; Tom, Betsy, Carolyn and Julie for their support and patience while our work was in progress.

John Ferns,
McMaster University.

1

Introduction

Coming to Lucy Maud Montgomery's poetry for the first time I was rather surprised by its relative simplicity of style and lack of ornate poetic diction. It resembles more the simpler lyrics of Longfellow than the heavier style of the pre-Raphaelites and some of our Canadian "Confederation Poets."

The freshness of much of Montgomery's verse is perhaps best explained by the remarkable correlation between the markets she wrote for and her own loves and enthusiasms. The magazines wanted poems about fishing boats and storms at sea. She was born and bred within walking distance of the Gulf of St. Lawrence and always loved all the moods of the sea and shore. The magazines wanted poems about spring and meadows and woods. She loved the outdoors and spent most of her free time among trees, brooks, and fields. Thus she was not obliged to tear at her hair in order to meet the editors' requirements.

Montgomery wrote verse in large quantity and in varying quality. Well over five hundred of her poems appeared in contemporary magazines. The peak of this activity was from 1893-1916, that is, chiefly during her twenties and thirties. Her verse possesses many of the same features as her prose writing, and demonstrates her characteristic interests in the world of nature, human and family relationships, and stages of life.

Poetry began for her as a natural, almost instinctive passion, given more impetus by her lack of free communication with close family members or suitable companions. Eventually it became a tool usable for an introduction into the wider world or into the marketplace. But it always retained a confessional element for her, and its importance as an avenue of self-expression remained, especially when the novel became her dominant public medium. This explains, in part, why her earlier poetry is somewhat fresher, before it had become more of a product for the market, and why as she grew older she returned to poetry again to express some of her deeper feelings.

She herself sometimes expressed a preference for her poetry over her prose. She wrote to G. B. MacMillan in 1903: "I don't know whether I call verse my specialty or not. I know that I touch a far higher note in my verse than in prose. But I write much more prose than verse because there is a wider market for it, especially among the juvenile publications." As time went on the growing demand for her fiction squeezed out more of the time she wished to give to verse.

Readers of Late Romantic verse are often distressed by the rather uninspired nature and repetitiveness of much of it. Poems on certain favoured topics — the sea, the seasons, the innocence of childhood, the old homestead, the triumph of hard work — were often used as fillers by popular magazines of the period. These verses tended to be organized on rather simple lines in order to be readily understood by a large and fairly unsophisticated audience. Poems frequently were of three or four stanzas — each stanza representing a different aspect of the theme. In a poem describing a scene in nature, for example, the three stanzas might describe its appearance at morning, noon, and evening respectively, or a four stanza poem might sketch the same scene during each of the seasons.

The long-term effect of producing large quantities of verse on a limited number of subjects was often a vague and general style which took refuge in "poetical" phrasing and literary platitudes. Poets such as Tennyson and Masefield who attempted to write verses every day showed a progressive decline in poetic verve and expressiveness. Montgomery is no exception to the rule that the demand for quantity rather than quality eventually showed itself in repetitiveness and undistinguished work. Since, however, she switched her energies to prose fairly early in her career the effects are not as blatant as with some other writers. Although she does have a few favourite "poetical" words such as "adown" and "athwart" such poeticisms are usually limited, especially in her earlier poetry.

It is worth repeating, in any case, that the modernist scorn for poetic diction is not well-founded. Since the time of Homer and Hesiod the majority of poets have written in a language which was not that of contemporary conversation. Our current habit, therefore, of dismissing any language except street-talk and journalese as stilted or unnatural detracts unnecessarily from our pleasure in reading poetry from all literary periods. Certain periods, such as Montgomery's own, added a large number of poetic and literary words to ordinary speech. It is interesting to find our author using the same poetical terms in her diary descriptions of nature as she uses in her verse. Her diary for 12 September 1891 (when she was nearly seventeen) tells us that "we sat down to rest and fell into a reverie. I gazed dreamily down the vistas. The yellow sunshine fell lazily athwart the tall gray spruces and the gossamers glimmered like threads of silver among the trees." Readers of her novels will recall similar passages.

Perhaps in the lack of detailed description in her nature verse there is a sign that a generalizing impetus has had some effect. And even in the present selection of poems ample evidence of repetition will be found. This, however, may be partly due to the limitations of Montgomery's physical circumstances, which barred her from a wider range of activities and experiences. Elizabeth Epperly speaks of this "penchant for repetition" as it occurs in the novels: "Again and again in the twenty L. M. Montgomery novels we find these words and images: spicy scent of ferns, tricksy winds, apple-green sunset skies, the fragrance of trampled mint." Such reiteration does not enhance her verse, although, as Epperly says, it works well enough in prose. It does show where her heart lay.

Besides casting a poetic glow over nature, Montgomery shows the related tendency of humanizing it. On the last day of 1892 she wrote in her diary: "'92 dies tonight — a glorious death, for the white earth floats in aerial silver of frost and moonshine and the sky is powdered with thousands of stars to watch its deathbed." In her poetry she frequently uses the method of Shelley's poem "The Cloud" in which an object in nature addresses the reader.

Some of Montgomery's favourite poets were pantheistic, that is, they tended to believe that all things were indwelt by, and were part of, the Divine Nature: She herself favoured this belief, and the tendency to speak of nature in the language of religion is very common in her own verse. We read, for example, in her poem "After Drought":

> The saintly meadow lilies offer up
> Their white hearts to the sun,
> And every wildwood blossom lifts its cup
> With incense overrun;
> The brook whose voice was silent yestereve

Now sings its old refrain,
And all the world is grateful to receive
The blessing of the rain.

Expressing one order of experience in terms of another has commonly been an essential part of the poetic tradition.

For Montgomery writing poetry was more than a literary activity: it was almost a form of Holy Communion. To read poetry was to glimpse into the realm of ideal beauty. God spoke to man through Poetry and Nature. In this trinity God was the most remote and inscrutable member. Indeed, because we only see God darkly through his creation and the writings of great men, all dogmas (said the transcendentalists) are merely human products. The poet is then a kind of priest who interprets the universe to men, who unfortunately are often not wise enough to acclaim his insights.

There was a distinct element of snobbery in this new pantheistic religion, for in order to be a transcendentalist it was almost a requirement to be either a writer or an artist. Montgomery herself often wrote sarcastically about the homely Presbyterianism of her background, although she carefully maintained the forms of Christianity all her life. Jesus was merely transformed into a wise and poetical teacher — one of the many precursors of Emerson. One unfortunate effect of the prevalence of transcendentalism in literary circles was a distinct division of everything into either beautiful, poetical, spiritual, and intellectual or ugly, commonplace, materialistic, and stupid. Most aspects of the world around us, including people and institutions, tended to fall into the latter group. Among people only a few "kindred spirits" transcended the usual prosaic modes of existence. The poet was foremost among those who aspired to a truer and more beautiful life and scorned the mundane realities of everyday living. Montgomery approvingly quoted Emerson on ideal *versus* real life: "In the actual — this painful kingdom of time and chance — are Care, Canker and Sorrow: with thought, with the ideal, is immortal hilarity — the rose of joy; round it all the Muses sing."

It is easy to see how such a philosophy could fall into a rather self-indulgent escapism, and this is sometimes the case in her poetry. It also provided the seeds for developing an aloof, critical, and even hostile attitude toward people in general. Such an attitude is quite apparent in some of her later novels such as *Mistress Pat*.

Because poetry is more demanding than prose certain weaknesses show up in Montgomery's verse which are not very noticeable in her fiction. A scattering of clumsy sentences will often be skimmed over in a novel, while a single awkward or imprecise word may damage a short poem.

Even some of Montgomery's briefer poems continue when the inspiration has been exhausted. She was not a disciplined student of the art of verse and her composition habits remained haphazard throughout her career. She would, for example, write the rough draft of a poem first, and then go back over it adding rhymes. The result is that her rhyming is sometimes a pyrrhic victory over sense and syntax. The poem "An Autumn Shower" illustrates this in lines which describe the wind as coming

> To croon in minstrel grasses; where it stirs
> The goldenrod its kingly vesture wears.

No adjustment of punctuation can turn this into English. The author evidently wanted to say that the wind "stirs the goldenrod," but was faced then with finding a suitable rhyme for "stirs" and failed. Such poor phrasing detracts from an otherwise agreeable poem.

It is a pleasing irony that the modern "Can. Lit." movement, which began as an attack on traditional literature, is now sponsoring the careful editing of these same works of the past. This is because the literature industry has now grown too large to subsist solely on the writings of the declared modernists from F. R. Scott to Margaret Atwood. The result of this unconscious revisionism has been to open our eyes anew to some standard authors who received rather short shrift from critics of the last generation.

Montgomery was a favourite target of the once "New Critics" both on account of the date of her birth and her popularity. Since she began writing before T.S. Eliot, Ezra Pound and D.H. Lawrence became the established literary models, and because her books were intended to be popular and were so, she offended both in style and subject matter. She herself was an unashamed opponent of the modernist movement, as readers of her lines on "vers libre" will discover.

The re-discovery of Montgomery, therefore, is a phenomenon in our literary history which opens our eyes both to the processes of neglect and restoration. An entire generation of poets who were omitted from such collections as Margaret Atwood's *New Oxford Book of Canadian Verse* are resurfacing due to a combination of academic industry and popular interest. Some Canadian critics who have felt that "things in general were settled for ever" may find this little to their liking. Others will wonder why this bulk of often admittedly mediocre verse needs to be reexamined. We hope that this volume will provide at least a partial explanation.

In spite of growing critical rejection Montgomery has continued to be perhaps the most popular of Canadian fiction writers, not only in Canada, but throughout Europe, the United States, and Japan. This popularity, however, has been based almost solely on her novels, and, in particular, the *Anne of Green Gables* series. She has been persistently typecast as the writer of one good children's book who continued to work the same vein with diminishing returns. Until recently no attempt was made to collect her short stories (numbering over five hundred), and these were rarely anthologized, and indeed rarely mentioned. In the same way her poetry (apart from the bare fact that a collection had once been published) fell almost entirely from view.

This collection published in 1916 as *The Watchman and Other Poems*, made comparatively small sales, and its failure with the general public of the day is curious. The author was already a very popular writer and her book received largely favourable reviews. It may be that (as was often her fate) her poetry fell between the cracks. Her verse was even then rather old-fashioned and too lacking in urgency or "high seriousness" to appeal to the devotees of literature. On the other hand it was perhaps too serious and literary to appeal to the majority of her readers. Largely because of its small circulation, *The Watchman* has, in recent times, become something of a collector's item.

Lucy Maud Montgomery was born on 30 November 1874 in Clifton, Prince Edward Island. She was descended on both sides from Scottish stock settled on the Island for several generations, except for her English-born maternal grandmother. The significance of being sprung from the "first families" of Cavendish and the Island was not lost on some of Montgomery's relatives, and perhaps not on herself. Shortly after she was born her mother, Clara Macneill, developed tuberculosis, and died when the little girl was 22 months old. Hugh John Montgomery, the author's father, tried a variety of jobs to make a living, and decided at last, when his daughter was six, to go west to Saskatchewan to try his fortune there. On her mother's death Lucy Maud had been left in the care of her maternal grandparents Alexander and Lucy Woolner Macneill of Cavendish, P.E.I.

The death of a parent, and particularly a mother, during the first three years of a child's life may have a permanent negative effect on the personality. A lifelong tendency toward depression, nervous anxiety, and insecurity may be linked to such a loss. This certainly was the case with Maud Montgomery. She was, like her heroines, an orphan, for she saw her father only twice after he left P.E.I. — once when she was nine, and again for a year during her teens. He died in Saskatchewan in 1900, when she was twenty-five. She always regarded her father very affectionately, although he had little direct influence on her upbringing or material circumstances.

The responsibility of raising the little girl fell, therefore, almost entirely on the grandparents, who no doubt regarded the task rather as a duty than a pleasure. As they grew older the strain between them and their charge also grew, until it illustrated the Elizabethan maxim that "crabbed age and youth cannot live together." The Macneills had already raised six children, and, being now in their fifties, were interested chiefly in a quiet life. As the girl got older her desire for society and her grandparents' desire for solitude were in frequent conflict. It is perhaps significant that many of her earliest recollections were painful ones, but it is also possible that she partly reconstructed her childhood to suit later moods of depression.

Regarding her grandparents, she wrote to G. B. MacMillan in 1905: "In material respects they were good and kind to me and I am sincerely grateful to them. But in many respects they were unwise in their treatment of me . . . I was shut out from all social life . . . and debarred from the companionship of other children and — in early youth — other young people. I had *no* companionship except that of books and solitary rambles in wood and fields." Even with respect to books the Macneill home did not provide many companions. There were few novels or magazines, and Montgomery learned early to revel in poetry. Longfellow, Tennyson, Whittier, Scott, Byron, Milton, and Burns were read and reread and became part of her world. She remained true to her first loves and, years later (February 1896), when she received her first cheque for her writing she used the money to buy books of poetry by five of these authors. Her sincere appreciation for some often rather middling poets — Longfellow, Whittier, Scott, Ingelow, Hemans — no doubt aided her contentment in following the same path herself.

She recollected having written her first verses when she was nine, and first submitting a poem to an editor at the age of twelve. In August

1890 (at age fifteen) Montgomery journeyed by train to Prince Albert, Saskatchewan, to live with her father and his second wife. She stayed there one year and her experiences in the new setting and her regular correspondence with friends at home seem to have given considerable impetus to her writing. That year also saw her first appearance in print — a narrative poem entitled "On Cape Le Force" printed in the Charlottetown *Daily Patriot* on 26 November 1890. Before the year was out she had several more pieces in print which reinforced her passion for writing. The attempt to be reunited with her father, however, was at best a partial success largely because of her step-mother's hostility which she came to reciprocate. She gladly went back to Cavendish in August 1891. The verses from this year show considerable technical ability and human interest, but also a certain bookishness and verbal infelicity.

Montgomery continued her writing back in P.E.I., although she also gave heed to preparing herself to teach in the local schools. In 1893 (at age 18) she first broke into the wider North American literary market with a poem in *The Ladies' World,* a popular American magazine for women. The two subscriptions which she received in payment for this poem were the first tangible reward for her writing.

After one happy year of teaching school at Bideford, P.E.I., Montgomery decided to further her education by a year at Dalhousie College in Halifax. This year (1895-96) was both an academic and literary success, and marks a new era in her self-confidence and literary verve. In one week of February 1896 work of hers was accepted by three different editors and for all three pieces she was paid. Perhaps the proudest achievement was the acceptance of her poem "Fisher Lassies" by the *Youth's Companion,* possibly the leading juvenile publication in America, and the resulting cheque for twelve dollars.

The work accepted that week showed considerable competence, and a growing talent for making the most of any theme or suggestion. Her verses on "Which has the most patience under ordinary cares and trials of life — man or woman?" are worth including in this collection for their new freedom in thought and expression.

Montgomery returned to school-teaching in P.E.I. for the next two years, but with a renewed determination to succeed in the literary world. She began rising early each morning in order to get in some time for writing. These years (1896-98) were productive of much good verse, and Montgomery gradually added new names to the list of journals accepting her work. The death of her grandfather in March 1898 required her return to Cavendish to care for her grandmother and her property. She remained at Cavendish with her grandmother till the latter's death in March 1911, except for one job as reporter-writer for the Halifax *Daily Echo* from October 1901 till June 1902. In Cavendish she continued to write poetry but began concentrating more on prose because of the larger market for it, and her need to supplement the limited family income. The death of her father in 1900 was a great blow to her hopes and perhaps accounts partly for the gloomy forebodings which recur in her diaries during her later years in Cavendish.

Her work on the *Daily Echo* may have had a negative effect on the freshness and individuality of her poetry. In Halifax she taught herself to write verse amidst all the noises and distractions of a newspaper office. Her friend Ephraim Weber admired her ability to write a poem like "Sea Gulls" in a printing office. Yet we may wonder if her talent for producing something to order on any subject wasn't stretched too far.

After 1901 Montgomery's verse seems increasingly to rely on generalized memories and technical facility rather than on direct and immediate feelings or impressions. At any rate we find more and more literary touches in her poems which we might wish away and fewer markedly individualized sentiments. By 1906 it is not uncommon to find her writing such garishly poetical posings as the following piece entitled "Twilight":

> From vales of dawn hath Day pursued the Night
> Who mocking fled, swift-sandalled, to the west,
> Nor ever lingered in her wayward flight
> With dusk-eyed glance to recompense his guest,
> But over crocus hills and meadows gray
> Sped fleetly on her way.
>
> Now when the Day, shorn of his failing strength,
> Hath fallen spent before the sunset bars,
> The fair, wild Night, with pity touched at length,
> Crowned with her chaplet of out-blossoming stars,
> Creeps back repentantly upon her way
> To kiss the dying Day.

Another factor was at work which may be noted in the verses of many middling poets. They often begin by writing about what they know and their own experiences, but gradually those scenes, ideas, and incidents which are of real interest to the writer and have real literary possibilities are used up. Then the poet's work tends to become increasingly repetitive and starts to compensate by verbal dexterity and literary ingenuity for the absence of fresh inspiration. It is at this point that Montgomery turned more and more to prose and, in fact, began to write what later became *Anne of Green Gables*.

Many of the poems which she wrote between 1891 and 1911 reflect the life she lived in Cavendish and are the more interesting for that. As one one of her stronger talents lay in evoking the past, she continued to use these memories in her poems and novels. A typical early poem is "The Gable Window" (published 1897) which begins:

It opened on a world of wonder,
When summer days were sweet and long:
A world of light, a world of splendor,
A world of song.

'Twas there I passed my hours of dreaming,
'Twas there I knelt at night to pray:
And, when the rose-lit dawn was streaming
Across the day

I bent from it to catch the glory
Of all those radiant silver skies —
A resurrection allegory
For human eyes!

The summer raindrops on it beating,
The swallows clinging 'neath the eaves,
The wayward shadows by it fleeting,
The whispering leaves . . .

In such a poem she was able to combine real experience with her love for dreaminess and evocation of the past.

Her early nature poetry also has an energy sometimes lacking in her later work, as in these lines from "In Haying Time" (published 1897):

The fields at dawn are silver-white,
And wet with their baptismal dew;
They ripen in the long, rare noons,
Beneath a dome of cloudless blue.
And in the twilight's purple dusk,
How solemn, hushed, and dim they lie!

At night the mellow moon looks down
From silent, star-sown depths of sky.

Each passing hour of night and day
Some new and rare enchantment brings,
In flowers that bloom and winds that blow,
And joy of shy, blithe living things
That hide within the meadows green,
Or murmur in the drowsy fields;
And all the golden air is sweet
With incense rose-red clover yields.

The demand for her stories, serials, and novels took away most of her time for writing verse. On 10 November 1907 she wrote to Ephraim Weber: "Do you know I haven't written a single line of verse since July. I'm going to try to write a poem tomorrow." Following the publication and success of *Anne of Green Gables* (1908) she turned increasingly to writing novels, resolving to give up all "hack work." She had little trouble now publishing her verses and in 1916 brought out the collection entitled *The Watchman and Other Poems*.

As with some other poets Montgomery was not the most judicious editor of her own work. *The Watchman* contains a disproportionate number of poems of the "Twilight" variety, in which the straining to be poetic is rather too obvious. At the same time the collection omits many of her earlier simpler nature lyrics which make up good part of her best work. Only one of the ten poems which make up the section "The World of Nature" in the present volume comes from *The Watchman*. Without attempting to exclude poems from *The Watchman* from their own collection, the present editors found that the correlation between their selections and Montgomery's own was very small.

She continued to write verse almost up to her death, and took great pleasure in her work. One later poem which shows both inspiration and technical maturity is "Night" (published 1935):

A pale, enchanted moon is sinking low
Behind the dunes that fringe the shadowy lea,
And there is haunted starlight on the flow
Of immemorial sea.

I am alone and need no more pretend
Laughter or smile to hide a hungry heart,

I walk with solitude as with a friend
Enfolded and apart.

We tread an eerie road across the moor
Where shadows weave upon their ghostly looms,
And winds sing an old lyric that might lure
Sad queens from ancient tombs.

The distinction which Montgomery made between herself and others in her neighbourhood is hinted at when she writes of her neighbours' response to *Anne of Green Gables:* "If you have lived all your life in a little village where everybody is every whit as good and clever and successful as everybody else, and if you are foolish enough to do something which the others in the village cannot do, especially if that something brings you in a small modicum of fame and fortune, a certain class of people will take it as a personal insult to themselves, will belittle you and your accomplishment in every way and will go out of their way to make sure that you are informed of their opinions." She often contrasts the beauty of nature with the drabness of the lives she sees around her. She rarely can detail any spark of spirituality or glimmer of romance or intellect in her neighbours or in their faith and thought. "As a rule", she writes, "I am very careful to be shallow and conventional where depth and originality are wasted. When I get very desperate I retreat into my realms of cloudland and hold delightful imaginary dialogues with the shadowy, congenial shapes I meet there."

As with many Romantic writers and some of their modern descendants, she sometimes seems to put a higher premium on writing well than on living well. Energy which she could well have used in her everyday living, especially as she grew older, was applied towards her next poem, story, or novel. She tried to put herself into her work and often succeeds better than one would expect. Although she confessed disbelief in the deity of Jesus, her poems on the incarnation and resurrection are by no means without feeling, or mere formal exercises. Her imaginative power sometimes flashes forth in the unlikeliest places and often gives a brief splendour to even the weakest parts of her work.

"A house divided against itself cannot stand." As a young adult Montgomery lived two separate lives. On the one hand she was the dutiful and caring granddaughter, the church organist and Sunday School teacher, and the highly respectable and well-principled young lady, whose name was often mentioned to bachelor clergymen as an eligible wife. On the other hand she was often the nervous, fearful, unhappy, angry and critical young woman who confided her complaints, heresies, hatreds, ambitions, and discontents with her whole manner of life to her diary and a few favoured correspondents.

From an early age she had feelings of being an outsider among her mother's relatives, and later expressed a decided preference for her father's family. There seems to have been a marked difference of temperament between her and her closest Macneill relatives. As she grew older the thoughts of slights and criticisms which she had received as a child from the Macneill clan were a recurring source of bitterness. Her grandfather, unfortunately, was much given to teasing and rough jocular personal remarks which were taken to heart by the young girl. Her grandmother, while not unkind, was too formal and restrained in her relations with her granddaughter to provide much compensation for the loss of a father and mother. When she became a young woman she resented the restricted social and emotional life of her grandparents, and developed an unhealthy preoccupation with the disadvantages of her childhood, adolescence, and young adulthood.

Impressions made at an early age, before reason is well-developed, are largely immune to later modification. Maturity and rationality generally provide plausible reasons for early likes and dislikes, and help to enhance and nurture childhood prejudices. The feelings of discomfort and distaste which Montgomery sometimes felt as a child for her immediate surroundings only grew deeper as she grew older, and, by an association of ideas, tended to embrace whatever was connected with her early memories. For example, churchgoing for her became mainly a social activity because it provided an escape from her home surroundings, and gave her a taste of society. On the other hand the imagery and doctrines of Christianity were forever associated by her with her grandparents and their contemporaries and, therefore, aroused a generally negative response. Her diary comments that her Sunday School teachers "rather prejudiced me against it, since they were 'Christians' and I somehow had the idea that to be a Christian meant to be as ugly and stupid and — well, as unromantic as those 'good' women were."

Her early insecurities are probably one reason why she had difficulty finding emotional satisfaction all through her life. Her reluctance to take risks, including to risk doing what she really wanted to do, is perhaps related to this lack of self-confidence. Thus she remained for many years the nurse and housekeeper for her grandmother, even though the latter had had six children of her own. She was only deeply in love once, and backed away from this involvement, giving herself plausible but perhaps fallacious reasons for doing so. When she did marry it was more an affair of the head than the heart, and her husband proved to have more emotional problems than she did. Later on she made an urgent deal with her publisher in order to get some ready money and so deprived herself of very handsome royalties for years to come. She became engaged afterwards in a long and bitter lawsuit with the same publisher, partly perhaps because of her vexation about this blunder.

Wounds are no less painful for being self-inflicted. She fled from these hurts to her diary, her correspondents, her writing, her cats, the world of nature, and a few favourite friends and family members. Like others who have lost parents and other near relations she developed an interest in spiritualism, psychic phenomena, life after death, and reincarnation. She felt personally the horror and tragedy of World War I, and the approach of World War II filled her with dread. The pressures of social isolation, literary success, caring for her grandmother (and later her husband), coping with her own and her family's problems and playing the role of a minister's wife took their toll, and she suffered periods of nervous exhaustion throughout her adult life. Writing became more and more important to her as a proof of vitality, and an escape from worry.

Montgomery's pursuit of literary success was perhaps partly motivated by a desire to convince both her family and herself of her own value. To her correspondent Ephraim Weber she never tires of enumerating the magazines which accept her work, and how much they pay. In her first letter to G. B. MacMillan she proudly tells him how much she earns by writing, although she would have been shocked if one of her neighbours had asked her about it. The only way which she could justify to her family, her community and even to herself her passion for writing was by earning money from it, and she set out doggedly to accomplish this.

Montgomery belonged to "Young America" when pioneering was still a contemporary phenomenon and urbanization could still be overlooked. Her generation was perhaps the last to be dominated by rural or small-town writers. Archibald Lampman grew up in small Ontario towns such as Morpeth, Perrytown, Gore's Landing, and Cobourg. Charles G. D. Roberts spent his most impressionable years in Westcock, N.B., while

Wilfred Campbell lived in Wiarton, Ontario, for some years. Wilson MacDonald was born in Cheapside, and Pauline Johnson grew up a few miles from Brantford, Ont. The chief centres of Canadian writing at the turn of the century were Fredericton N.B., and Ottawa.

The total lack of sympathy between these Late Romantics and the modernist school results partly from this rural-urban split. Modernism in poetry derives almost entirely from the metropolitan centres — Paris, London, New York, and Chicago — and its chief practitioners have little experience of or interest in the world of nature. Such leaders as T.S. Eliot and Ezra Pound were in fact expatriates. Modernism naturally took as its chief theme the alienation of urban man, thus invoking its own nemesis. When modernism reached Canada it gravitated to the largest centres — Montreal and Toronto — from where it carried on warfare against the tradition of nature poetry and popular verse.

The split between Late Romanticism and Modernism was also one of feeling *versus* intellect. The Romantics loved poetry partly as a way of expressing their feelings, and as a mode of vicariously enjoying the feelings of others. Montgomery wrote to G. B. MacMillan regarding her admiration for Robert Burns: "What a magnificent creature he was! I've loved his poetry ever since I was a baby. A great many poets appeal only or almost only to the intellect. Burns appeals to the heart and in this I think is the secret of his power. He makes his verses *live* with the richness of his own nature . . . He gave voice to the song that sings itself in *all* human hearts . . ."

Another barrier which divides Modernism from Late Romanticism is the growth of academicism in literature, creating an artificial audience which makes the general reader redundant. Montgomery's generation was already feeling the tightening of the screws, and she herself spent a year at Dalhousie College, Halifax in hopes of enhancing her literary prospects. The traditional position that poetry must give pleasure to the general reader has thus been outflanked by the rapid growth of English and Modern Language Studies and the establishment of groups of scholar-critics whose reading is motivated more by career goals than by pleasure in reading. It is, therefore, no longer necessary that an author's work possess any generally appreciated qualities for it to be esteemed a critical success. The focus of modern literature, indeed, lies rather on the ingenuity of its professional audience than on the abilities of the writers themselves.

Montgomery's own best poetry is usually an overflow of her feelings or an expression of her moods. A good example of this are the rhymes which express her joy on the birth and infancy of her first son Chester. Further inspired by a visit of her dear friend, Fredericka Campbell, the two conspired to write humorous verses: "Frede and I have such fun in the mornings when I bathe and dress him in the kitchen while she is washing the breakfast dishes. We talk the most delicious nonsense to him, make all the funny impromptu rhymes we can about him, and act the fool generally, none daring to make us afraid. Here for example is this morning's classic on "The Pirate Wag" — which is one of Frede's nicknames for him:

> There was a pirate known as Wag
> Whose Sunday name was Punch;
> He sailed upon the raging main
> And ate his aunts for lunch.
>
> He liked them fricasseed and stewed;
> But sometimes for a change,
> He broiled them nice and tenderly
> Upon his kitchen range.
>
> But he preferred them piping hot
> Served up in a tureen,
> Fried in deep fat a golden brown
> And decked with parsley green.
>
> And when an aunt was saucier
> Than usual Waggy said,
> 'I'll have you made into a hash
> You gristly old Aunt Frede.'

It is difficult for us to even imagine the importance of poetry to Montgomery and many of her contemporaries, and its unquestioned role in their lives. She describes the visit of an old friend to her home — they had been school-mates forty or so years earlier — and wrote of their happy reunion: "Sometimes we quoted poetry. Nora would voice the first line of a couplet and I would finish it. Once in this alternate way we recited the whole of Wordsworth's Ode on the Intimations of Immortality, lingering over the lines 'Our birth is but a sleep and a forgetting etc.' " Poetry was at the centre of her life and when we read her verses with this in mind it illuminates both her own experience and that of the era in which she lived.

Montgomery herself kept a list of her published poems and the amounts which she was paid for them. While evidently it omits some of her earlier work, it provides a good basis for a bibliography of her poetry, listing 516 of her poems. She kept scrapbooks of much of her published work and photocopies of these were passed on to her bibliographer, Rea Wilmshurst of Toronto. At length, when Miss Wilmshurst had collected some 454 of the poems, they were sent to the present editors. We also received an additional thirteen poems printed only in *The Watchman,* and eight other poems from the manuscript which was published as *The Road to Yesterday.* Since then some twenty other poems have turned up in various locations.

Barring the discovery of a major cache of Montgomery manuscripts, it would seem that the vast majority of her verse has been accounted for. This selection provides nearly one-fifth of this total, and was chosen to display both what is best and what is typical in her work.

Until her collected work appears it seems rather premature to attempt to sum up her status as a poet. The main outlines, however, are fairly clear. Her work compares favourably with that of such contemporaries as Pauline Johnson and Robert Service. It is based on popular models and intended for a popular audience; its distinction lies in being written with somewhat more talent, individuality, and feeling than the bulk of the verse of its day. Since verse of a popular kind has largely ceased to be written, or, at least, published within the literary establishment, these Late Romantic writers will continue to supply an audience brought up in the Romantic tradition.

By working back through Late Romanticism we can once again draw up the threads which lead us back to the seamless garment of English Poetry as it existed in the days of Spenser, Shakespeare, Jonson, Donne, Herrick, and Milton. The qualities of great poetry remain the same, but they must be realized anew for each generation, or else the tradition falters.

It remains true that half a poet is better than none. The weakened verse of the Late Romantic tradition is nonetheless to be valued for reasons other than those for the non-poetry or anti-poetry of today. It can claim some of the praises which Hesiod, one of the fathers of Western literature, bestows upon the bard in the *Theogony* (11. 96-103):

And he is happy whom the Muses love.
Sweet words flow from his lips. And if someone
Is sorrowful in mind, and grieved in heart,
Still, when the poet, servant of the Muse,
Recites the glorious deeds of olden men
And sings the blessed gods of high Olympus,
At once that man is freed from heavy cares,
And sorrows are forgotten, while the gifts
Of heavenly Muses entertain his thoughts.

Kevin McCabe
University of Regina

Part I

Poems of Nature

The Mayflower's Message

Here on the gray old hillside where minstrel breezes blow,
And fir-trees dim and ancient with mossy branches grow,
'Mid grasses brown and broken where scarce our faces show,
All bravely and undaunted we bloom above the snow.

The winds are chill and bitter that o'er the valleys ring,
And not a vagrant bluebird as yet is here to sing;
But all the world is waiting to greet the news we bring,
And all our blossoms letter a message from the spring.

We are the blithe forerunners of sunshine and of May,
And many a wood-bird's rondel and many a merry day.
Therefore, sad earth, we bid you all joyous be and gay,
For we are sent to tell you that springtime comes this way.

Apple Blossoms

White as the snows on sunless peaks,
  Pink as the earliest blush of morn,
Pure as the thought of a stainless soul,
  Perfect and sweet as a joy new-born:
Always they bloom in these long rare days,
  When Maytime drifts into balmy June,
When the winds purr lightly among the leaves,
  And meadow and woodland are all atune;
Ever and always there they blow —
Apple-blossoms of rose and snow!

Purple twilights and rose-red dawns,
  Dimmest of hazes on far green hills,
Wonderful midnights and clear blue days,
  Rapturous music of wild-bird trills:
Lightness of heart and dreams of joy,
  Subtlest visions and fancies fair,
Tenderest hopes for the hours to come,
  Freedom from worry and grief and care:
Come where the apple-blossoms blow —
Perfumed driftings of rose and snow.

In Lilac Time

When the hills in the distance are misty
With hazes of shimmering blue,
When the birds sing with rapture at dawning
And the pastures are silver with dew,
When the skies are of sapphire radiance
And the apple tree boughs are ablow,
Then the lilacs hang out in the garden
Their clusters of purple and snow.

When a new moon shines after the sunset
In the heart of the mellow southwest,
And the winds astray in the meadows
Are bent on their summertime quest,
When the cherry trees down in the orchard
Are white as the robe of a bride,
The lilac trees here at my window
Are decked in their splendor and pride.

In the odorous hush of the twilight
The evening breeze steals their perfume,
Till the rain-freshened nooks of the garden
Are sweet with the breath of their bloom,
And at morning a bluebird a-tilting
On the tip of a tremulous spray
Pipes out in their thicket of sweetness
A madrigal buoyant and gay.

Oh! our hearts are atune with the music
Of summer and blossom and bird!
It is worth our while just to be living
When the pulses of nature are stirred.
There's nothing so sweet as the joyance
That comes when the June breezes blow
And the lilac trees out in the garden
Are crowned with their purple and snow.

In Haying Time

Wide meadows under lucent skies
  Lie open, free to sun and breeze,
  Where bird and bee and rustling leaf
  Blend all their air-born melodies
In one sweet symphony of sound.
  The lush green grasses bend and sway,
And fleet winds steal from new-mown slopes
  The fragrance of the clover hay.

The fields at dawn are silver-white,
  And wet with their baptismal dew;
They ripen in the long rare noons
  Beneath a dome of cloudless blue;
And in the twilight's purple dusk,
  How solemn, hushed, and dim they lie!
At night a mellow moon looks down
  From silent, star-sown, depths of sky.

Each passing hour of night and day
  Some new and rare enchantment brings,
In flowers that bloom and winds that blow,
  And joy of shy, blithe, living things
That hide within the meadows green,
  Or murmur in the drowsy fields;
And all the golden air is sweet
  With incense rose-red clover yields.

Faint whispers wander to and fro,
  On idle winds, from east to west.
The dainty blossoms lift their cups
  Of perfume o'er the bluebird's nest;
The meadowlarks their raptures trill
  To drown the brooklet's murmuring chime,
When ripened summer ushers in
  The witcheries of the haying time.

Out O' Doors

There's a gypsy wind across the harvest land,
Let us fare forth with it lightly hand in hand;
Where cloud shadows blow across the sunwarm waste,
And the first red leaves are falling, let us haste,
For the waning days are lavish of their stores,
And the joy of life is with us out o' doors!

Let us roam along the ways of goldenrod,
Over uplands where the spicy bracken nod,
Through the wildwood where the hemlock branches croon
Their rune-chant of elder days across the noon,
For the mellow air its pungency outpours,
And the glory of the year is out o' doors!

There's a great gray sea beyond us calling far,
There's a blue tide curling o'er the harbor bar;
Ho, the breeze that smites us salty on the lips
Whistles gaily in the sails of outbound ships;
Let us send out thoughts with them to fabled shores,
For the pilgrim mood is on us out o' doors!

Lo, the world's rejoicing in each spirit thrills,
Strength and gladness are to us upon the hills;
We are one with crimson bough and ancient sea,
Holding all the joy of autumn hours in fee,
Hope within us like a questing bird upsoars,
And there's room for song and laughter out o' doors!

An Autumn Shower

Upon the russet fringes of the hill
The shadow of a cloud falls dark and still;
Then with a sweep and rush of wind the rain
Comes down the valley and across the plain,
Where many a spicy cup
Of asters pale and sweet is lifted up.

The pattering feet of raindrops are astir
In pine-land aisles and resinous glens of fir,
And dance across the harbor till afar,
Beyond the restless moaning of the bar,
They croon in harmony
With all the harp-like voices of the sea.

The cloud is swift in passing — in an hour
The sun is shining on the parting shower
Athwart the flaming maples; and the cup
Of the long glistening valley is brimmed up
With wine of airy mist,
Purple and silver and faint amethyst.

The wind from many a wild untrodden bourne
Comes sweet with breath of drenched and tangled fern
To croon in minstrel grasses; where it stirs
The goldenrod its kingly vesture wears;
Meadow and wood and plain
Have caught the benediction of the rain!

When Autumn Comes

The city is around us, and the clamor of the mart:
Its grip is on our pulses, and its clutch upon our heart.
We cannot hear the music of the olden dreams and days:
We have no time to tread in thought the sweet forgotten ways.

But when the tang of autumn air sweeps up the breathless street,
With sudden hint of reddening leaves and garnered fields of wheat,
Of golden lights on pastures wide and shadows in the glen,
Our souls thrill with the yearning wish to be at home again.

Out there the misty sea laps glad on crisp and windy sands;
Out there the smoke-blue asters blow on breezy meadow lands;
Out there the joyous marigolds in marsh and swamp are bright —
Despite the breath of chilly morn and nip of frosty night.

The air is ripe and pungent, and the sky is free from stain;
The fallen leaves are whispering in many a woodland lane;
And O to roam upon the hills when all the west is red,
When the moon rises from the sea and stars shine overhead!

And O to see the homelight from the farmhouse window glow,
Athwart the purple-falling dusk as in the long ago;
To hail it with our eager eyes when pilgrimage is o'er,
And dream one dream of boyhood 'neath our father's roof
    once more!

The Last Bluebird

The grasses are sere and the meadows are brown,
The last clinging red leaf has fluttered adown;
The swallows and thrushes have long ago flown,
The woods are all voiceless, the valleys all lone,
    And soon I must flee
    Far over the sea
Where warm sunny southlands are waiting for me.

The sunsets are crimson, and all through the days
The tired earth is napping in magical haze;
But the mornings are frosty, the twilights are cold,
The woodways are lost in their driftings of gold,
    And well do I know
    That full soon comes the snow,
And in spite of the sunshine it's high time to go.

For the breath of the north wind is bitter and chill
And my nest-tree is bare on the slope of the hill:
Earth's music has fled, and the winter is long,
And over the sea I must follow my song;
    So I twitter good-by
    Once again ere I fly
To a far away land and a sunnier sky.

But the winter will pass, and once more in the spring
The violets will bloom and the robins will sing;
The orchards grow white, and the gay brooklets chime
Their welcome again to the fair summer time,
    And over the sea
    With a song glad and free,
I'll come back to my nest in the old apple tree.

The Lullaby

Today I walked on the uplands
  Where the vagrant breezes blow,
And I heard the autumn singing
  A lullaby soft and low,
As she tucked the flowers and grasses
  In a cradle warm and deep,
Like a loving nurse and tender,
  Crooning them all to sleep.

"The swallows are southward flying,"
  So ran the song I heard,
"And last night in the russet valley
  The breath of the frost-king stirred;
So you must sleep my darlings,
  While the drear days come and go,
Dreaming of springtide wakening
  Deep down under the snow.

"Goldenrod, you must slumber
  Here on the brown hill's crest;
Wood flowers all, you must nestle
  Close to the forest's breast;
Asters, clovers, and daisies,
  Warmly I fold you away —
In the wide kind arms of the meadows
  Sleep till the call of May.

Sleep till the swallows northward
   Come from across the sea,
And all the summer sunshine
   Laughs out o'er the windy lea.
Sleep, my dear little blossoms,
   While your slumber song I sing —
Sleep, little leaves and grasses
   And waken up in the spring.

November Dusk

A weird and dreamy stillness falls upon
  The purple breathless earth, the windless woods,
  The wimpling rims of valley solitudes,
The wide gray stubble-fields, and fallows wan —
A quiet hush, as if, her heyday gone,
  Tired Nature folded weary hands for rest
  Across the faded vesture of her breast,
Knowing her wintry slumbers hasten on.
Far and away beyond the ocean's rim
  The dull-red sunset fades into the gray
Of sombre wind-rent clouds, that marshal grim
  Around the closing portals of the day,
While from the margin of the tawny shore
Comes up the voice of waters evermore.

The First Snowfall

A bitter chill has fallen o'er the land
　In this dull breathlessness of afternoon:
Voiceless and motionless the maples stand,
　　Heart-broken, with each other to commune
In silent hopelessness. The cold gray sky
　　Has blotted out the mountain's misty blue,
The nearer hills are palled in sombre guise
　　Where shivering gleams of fitful light fall through.

Then comes the snowfall, as pale Autumn folds
　　A misty bridal veil about her hair,
And lingers waiting in the yellowed wolds
　　Until her wintry bridegroom greet her there.
The hills are hidden and we see the woods
　　Like hosts of phantoms in the waning light.
The grassless fields, the leaf-strewn solitudes,
　　Grow dim before the fast oncoming night.

The lonely meadows pale and whiten swift,
　　The trees their tracery of ermine weave,
Like larger flakes dim flocks of snowbirds drift
　　Across the fading landscape of the eve.
Darkness comes early and beneath its wings
　　We see a wraith-like world with spectres filled —
Naught but cold semblances of real things
　　As though Earth's breathing were forever stilled.

Buttercups

Like showers of gold dust on the marsh,
  Or an inverted sky,
The buttercups are dancing now
  Where silver brooks run by.
    Bright, bright,
    As fallen flakes of light,
      They nod
    In time to every breeze
That chases shadows swiftly lost
  Amid those grassy seas.

See, what a golden frenzy flies
  Through the light-hearted flowers!
In mimic fear they flutter now;
  Each fairy blossom cowers.
    Then up, then up,
    Each shakes its yellow cup
      And nods
    In careless grace once more —
A very flood of sunshine seems
  Across the marsh to pour.

Echo

Here in my bosky glen, beneath dim pines I hide,
Unseen by the curious eyes of men, alone in the hills I bide,
Where the sunrise is born and the cataract leaps down
    the mountain side.

Ever I wrap me round in my leafy solitude
With my gleaming wreath of myrtle crowned, in the depth of
    waste and wood,
To laugh at the world from the heart of the hills and mimic
    its every mood.

Dark are my eyes and hair, and my breast is white as snow,
But never a mortal may see how fair . . . I am fleeter than
    the roe,
And the silver notes of my mocking voice are all that the world
    may know.

You may hear me call at night, from the springs of haunted rills;
You may hear my laughter floating light, when the starry dew
    distils.
I am the nymph of the airy voice and my home is in the hills.

Whenever you call to me I will answer to you again;
But my form and face you will never see, you of the race of men,
I flee afar when you follow me to the heart of my purple glen!

The Pond Pasture

It is purely fair and fragrant in its wide unbroken green,
  Where the water laps and murmurs on the margin thick with fern;
All the slope is sweet and tangled with the clover's rose red screen,
  And the corners are a-flutter where the orange lilies burn.

There are countless shadows flying where the white-stemmed
    birches bend
  Over lisping wave and ripple on its hushed and dreamy shore.
There are minstrel breezes blowing where the swaying grasses blend,
  And the buttercups are rhyming all their golden fairy lore.

Here is always balm and healing for a world-worn, weary heart,
  Nature's hieroglyphic message that the centuries have conned;
Not a hint is here of striving or the turmoil of the mart —
  Just a world of rest and beauty in the pasture by the pond!

Drought

So long it is since kindly rain
　Fell on the thirsty meadow lands;
The birds forget their old refrain;
　The trees uplift their pleading hands
To hard bright skies that do not heed,
　But arch above the valley dim,
　And touch the far hill's burning rim,
And care not for our mighty need.

Athwart the dusty highway's glare
　The wan white daisies, drooping, lean;
The roses faint in their despair
　On pasture slopes no longer green;
The plaintive brooks have ceased to pray,
　Unfed by springs whose lips are dry,
　And the dull evening in the sky
Shuts out the brazen edge of day.

Great Father, listen to our prayer,
　And send on us Thy gracious rain
To hush the moan of our despair
　And drown the memory of our pain;
Then all the hills to Thee will raise
　A psalm of utter thankfulness;
　Thy name each thirsty blossom bless,
And every meadow hymn Thy praise.

After Drought

Last night all through the darkling hours we heard
  The voices of the rain,
And every languid pulse in nature stirred
  Responsive to the strain;
The morning brought a breath of strong sweet air
  From shadowy pinelands blown,
And over field and upland everywhere
  A new-born greenness shone.

The saintly meadow lilies offer up
  Their white hearts to the sun,
And every wildwood blossom lifts its cup
  With incense overrun;
The brook whose voice was silent yestereve
  Now sings its old refrain,
And all the world is grateful to receive
  The blessing of the rain.

Rain In The Country

Here in the country the cool sweet rain
Falls on the daisies and growing grain,
Shadows the pond with widening rings,
Kisses the lips of the lowland springs,
Plays with the pines on the hill-top dim
And fills the valley with mist abrim.

It splashes in shadowy forest nooks,
Dimples the faces of woodland brooks,
Whispers with leaves in untrodden ways,
Wraps the distance in sober grays,
Dances o'er meadows of lushest green
And scatters the petals where roses lean.

The Wood Pool

Here is a voice that soundeth low and far
  And lyric — voice of wind among the pines,
Where the untroubled, glimmering waters are,
  And sunlight seldom shines.

Elusive shadows linger shyly here,
  And wood-flowers blow, like pale sweet spirit-bloom;
And white slim birches whisper, mirrored clear
  In the pool's lucent gloom.

Here Pan might pipe, or wandering dryad kneel
  To view her loveliness beside the brim,
Or laughing wood-nymphs from the byways steal
  To dance around its rim.

'Tis such a witching spot as might beseem
  A seeker of young friendship's trysting-place,
Or lover yielding to the immortal dream
  Of one beloved face.

The Tree Lovers

They grew in the fringe of woodland at the foot of the
   homestead hill,
Where ran like a silver ribbon a dimpling summer rill —
A spruce and a leafy maple — so close together they grew
That hardly a lance of sunlight might pierce their greenness
   through.

Their mingled branches swaying cast ever a cooling shade
O'er the strip of emerald grassland where the happy children
   played,
And a slender lad and thoughtful, with dreamy eyes of blue,
Said the tree was a maple maiden and the spruce her lover true.

The fancy pleased the children, as fancies children will,
For it gave them a sense of friendship with the trees below the hill:
As if the spruce and the maple had a life to their own akin,
And beneath their bark imprisoned beat human hearts within.

They saw how the maple nestled to the spruce's sheltering side,
As his rugged green arms clasped her with fond protecting pride.
He was the taller and stronger; she the more graceful tree,
And never could human lovers more kind and faithful be.

When the winter snows were silver, and the winter winds
   were keen,
The gray-cloaked bride was leafless but the sturdy spruce
   was green;
And when the springtime rapture thrilled all the woodlands
   through,
The tender tints of maple were blent with his somber hue.

All through the days of summer they talked and whispered low,
While the gentle west-winds wavered their branches to and fro;
And in autumn the little maple, in her splendor of crimson gay,
Stood proudly close to her lover in his rugged and dark array.

The children have grown and wandered from the ken of the
    homestead hill,
But the trees through seasons many are green and faithful still.
Still nestles the little maple to her knightly lover's side,
And still the spruce-tree shelters with his mighty arms his bride,

Though the winter winds are biting, but the closer drawn are they,
As fond as when summer sunbeams among their branches play:
Time passes o'er them as lightly as it does o'er the ribbon rill,
There, as each season passes, at the foot of the homestead hill.

In Untrod Woods

Lonely, think you, this deep unbroken hush,
Unstirred save by leaf-murmurs or the rush
    Of fitful winds on-sweeping?
Nay, nay, not so! You have not learned the store
    Of deep enchantment that forever more
    These untrod woods are keeping.

They are not voiceless — in the night and day
Wood-whispers creep around and wood-winds stray
    In mossy beechen alleys,
And dusking pines are crooning evermore
Their mysteries of half-forgotten lore
    In sunlight-threaded valleys.

Slim birches lean o'er many a clear spring's heart,
As maidens viewing by themselves apart
    Their lissome charms reflected —
Now steals the chime of water murmurings,
And now some unseen woodbird's rondel sings,
    As sweet as unexpected.

The woods are never lonely, as I stray
Adown rain-freshened slopes I hear today
    All shy blithe forest voices,
Calling around me till the great wood's calm
Falls on my spirit with a wondrous balm,
    And my vexed heart rejoices.

The Wild Places

Oh, here is joy that cannot be
    In any market bought or sold,
    Where forests beckon fold on fold
In a pale silver ecstasy,
And every hemlock is a spire
Of faint moon-fire.

For music we shall have the chill
    Wild bugle of a vagrant wind
    Seeking for what it cannot find,
A lonely trumpet on the hill,
Or keening in the dear dim white
Chambers of night.

And there are colours in the wild:
    The royal purple of old kings;
    Rose-fire of secret dawn; clear springs
Of emerald in valleys aisled
With red pine stems; and tawny stir
Of dying fir.

And we shall know as lovers do
    The wooing rain, the eternal lure
    Of tricksy brook and beckoning moor,
The hidden laughters that pursue,
As if the gods of elder day
Were here at play.

For these wild places hold their own
    Boon myths of faun and goblin still,
    And have a lingering good-will
For folk in green if truth were known;
Oh, what an old delightful fear —
Hush, listen, hear!

Sunrise Along Shore

Athwart the harbor lingers yet
The ashen light of breaking day,
And where the guardian cliffs are set
The noiseless shadows skulk away,
But all the cloudless eastern sky
Is flushed with many a gracious hue,
And spears of light are piercing through
The ranks where huddled sea-mists fly.

Across the ocean, wan and gray,
Bright fleets of golden ripples come,
For at the birth-hour of the day
The roistering, wayward winds are dumb.
The rocks that stretch to meet the tide
Are smitten with a fiery glow,
And faint reflections come and go
Where fishing-boats at anchor ride.

All life leaps out to greet the light —
The shining sea-gulls dive and soar,
The swallows wheel in dizzy flight
The sandpeeps flit along the shore.
From every purple landward hill
The banners of the morning fly,
But on the headlands, dim and high,
The fishing hamlets slumber still.

One boat alone beyond the bar
Is sailing outward blithe and free,
To carry sturdy hearts afar
Across those wastes of shining sea,
To staunchly seek what may be won
From out the treasures of the deep,
To toil for those at home who sleep,
And be the first to greet the sun!

A Perfect Day

A day came up this morning o'er the sea —
Dawn-eyed and virgin from an orient shore —
And dear were the delights it brought to me,
   Dearer than any day had given before:
'Tis with sweet sorrow at the sunset bell
   I bid my day farewell.

For never, as I think, was light so fair
   On the green waves, and never rang so clear
The haunting elfin music of the air,
   And never fell so subtly on the ear
The antic pipes of freakish winds astir
   In bosky glens of fir.

The roses bloomed as if they only had
   One day of all the year on which to bloom,
And, bent on making wild and garden glad,
   Flung forth their long upgathering of perfume;
It seemed to me that every dappled hour
   Burst into lavish flower.

Then when the sunset came the rainbow west
   Was splendid, as if all days fair and good
Were at its portal to receive as guest
   My day into their purple sisterhood,
Crowning it on the ancient hills afar
   With an immortal star.

Forever shall it be a lyric page
   Of verse ambrosial, to be often conned,
Holding its treasure safe from touch of age
   Forever kept in a remembrance fond:
For this my day that came across the sea
   Brought heart's desire to me!

Requiem

Tonight, when the twilight fell,
  Died the beautiful Day!
  On the far dim hills she lay,
With her garland of asphodel —
Ring, wild winds, her knell.

Gems in her long dark hair
  Scattered the kindly Night;
  Over her bier the white
Clear stars are watching there —
Oh, the dead Day is fair!

Fair was she when she stood
  Poised on the hills of dawn,
  While their radiance over her shone
In the blithesome laughing mood
Of her mirthful maidenhood.

Fair was she then. Ah fair!
  But fairer is she now
  With the awful peace on her brow,
That only the dead may wear,
And the starlight on her hair.

Let us take our last farewell
  Of the beautiful calm-lipped Day,
  Ere the Night will hide her away
With a star for sentinel —
Ring, wild winds, her knell.

In Twilight Fields

O'er dewy meadows, dim and gray,
There comes a breath of balm,
And wilding slopes of far away
Are wrapped in pensive calm;
Afar the lustrous skies are deep,
And crystal planets shine,
Where roaming winds have dropped asleep
Among the hills of pine.

The daisies float above the grass,
Like spirits of the dew,
And low sweet voices faintly pass
The lush green thickets through.
Slow fades the mellow sunset light;
The dusker shadows creep;
Beneath the soothing touch of night
The world has found its sleep.

No echoes of the troubled day
Can stir this wondrous hour;
Noon's feverish breath is far away,
And care has lost its power.
Lulled on her broad maternal breast,
Our kind earth mother yields
A deep untainted peace and rest
In tranquil twilight fields.

Twilight In Abegweit

A filmy western sky of smoky red,
Blossoming into stars above a sea
Of soft mysterious dim silver spread
Beyond the long gray dunes' serenity:
Where the salt grasses and sea poppies press
Together in a wild sweet loneliness.

Seven slim poplars on the windy hill
Talk some lost language of an elder day,
Taught by the green folk that inhabit still
The daisied field and secret friendly way —
Forever keeping in their solitudes
The magic ritual of our northern woods.

The darkness woos us like a perfumed flower
To reedy meadow pool and wise old trees,
To beds of spices in a garden bower,
And the spruce valley's dear austerities;
I know their lure of dusk, but evermore
I turn to the enchantment of the shore.

The idle ships dream-like at anchor ride,
Beside the pier where wavelets lap and croon;
One ghostly ship sails outward with the tide
That swells to meet the pale imperial moon,
O fading ship, between the dark and light,
I send my heart and hope with you tonight.

Night In The Pastures

The night wind steals from the tranquil hills,
And its noiseless footsteps pass
O'er the dim hushed breadths of the pasture fields,
And the dew-wet trampled grass.
The stars are thick in the velvet sky,
Where a white young moon shines clear
Through the airy boughs of the poplars tall,
And the peace of the night is here.

The brook's soft gurgle is sweet and low,
And the sorrowful whip-poor-wills
Are grieving afar in the purple gloom
Of the dark encircling hills;
And the faint weird murmurs of elfin things
Through the shadowy pine-trees creep,
But the air is sweet with the hush of dreams,
And the fields have gone to sleep.

The placid cattle have laid them down
At the roots of the mystic firs,
And the sheep in the lowland are dimly white
Where the wind in the bracken stirs.
The hills are chanting a solemn hymn
At the altar of star and sky;
In a rapturous silence, a dim-lit calm,
The dewy pastures lie.

Here, in these meadows of starry rest,
In these mysteries of the night,
The manifold voices of Nature breathe
With a meaning of strange delight.
The passionless calm of the dreaming fields
Has the power of a holy prayer,
And the infinite love of the far dim hills
Shuts out every thought of care.

Night

A pale enchanted moon is sinking low
  Behind the dunes that fringe the shadowy lea,
And there is haunted starlight on the flow
  Of immemorial sea.

I am alone and need no more pretend
  Laughter or smile to hide a hungry heart;
I walk with solitude as with a friend
  Enfolded and apart.

We tread an eerie road across the moor
  Where shadows weave upon their ghostly looms,
And winds sing an old lyric that might lure
  Sad queens from ancient tombs.

I am a sister to the loveliness
  Of cool far hill and long-remembered shore,
Finding in it a sweet forgetfulness
  Of all that hurt before.

The world of day, its bitterness and cark,
  No longer have the power to make me weep;
I welcome this communion of the dark
  As toilers welcome sleep.

Midnight In Camp

Night in the unslumbering forest! From the free,
   Vast pinelands by the foot of man untrod,
Blows the wild wind, roaming rejoicingly
   This wilderness of God;
And the tall firs that all day long have flung
   Balsamic odors where the sunshine burned,
Chant to its harping primal epics learned
   When this old world was young.

Beyond the lake, white, girdling peaks uplift
   Untroubled brows to virgin skies afar,
And o'er the uncertain water glimmers drift
   Of fitful cloud and star.
Sure never day such mystic beauty held
   As sylvan midnight here in this surcease
Of toil, when the kind darkness gives us peace
   Garnered from years of eld.

Lo! Hearken to the mountain waterfall
   Laughing adown its pathway to the glen
And nearer, in the cedars, the low call
   Of brook to brook again.
Voices that garish daytime may not know
   Wander at will along the woody steeps,
And silent, silver-footed moonlight creeps
   Through the dim glades below.

Oh, it is well to waken with the woods
  And feel, as those who wait with God alone,
The forest's heart in these rare solitudes
  Beating against our own.
Close-shut behind us are the gates of care,
  Divinity enfolds us, prone to bless,
And our souls kneel. Night in the wilderness
  Is one great prayer.

On The Bay

When the salt wave laps on the long, dim shore,
   And frets the reef with its windy sallies,
And the dawn's white light is threading once more
   The purple firs in the landward valleys,
While yet the arms of the wide gray sea
Are cradling the sunrise that is to be,
The fisherman's boat, through the mist afar,
Has sailed in the wake of the morning star.

The wind in his cordage and canvas sings
   Its old glad song of strength and endeavor;
And up from the heart of the ocean rings
   A call of courage and cheer forever;
Toil and danger and stress may wait
Beyond the arch of the morning's gate,
But he knows that behind him, upon the shore,
A true heart prays for him evermore.

When a young moon floats in the hollow sky,
   Like a fairy shallop, all pale and golden,
And, over the rocks that are grim and high,
   The lamp of the lighthouse aloft is holden;
When the bay is like to a lucent cup,
With glamor and glory and glow filled up,
In the track of the sunset, across the foam,
The fisherman's boat comes sailing home.

The wind is singing a low, sweet song
　Of a rest well won and a toil well over,
And there on the shore shines clear and strong
　The star of the home light to guide the rover:
And deep unto deep may call and wail,
But the fisherman laughs as he furls his sail,
For the bar is passed and the reef is dim,
And a true heart is waiting to welcome him!

On The Gulf Shore

Lap softly on the curving shore
Where sandpeeps leave their footprints small;
Lap softly, purple waves, where o'er
The gleaming sand the ripples fall.
Aloft the sky is blue; the clouds
Are soft and white above the sea;
The seagulls fly in snowy crowds;
The boats are floating lazily.

Then lap, lap softly, purple waves!
No tempests toss your crests today —
Your azure dimples are the graves
Where millions buried sunbeams play.
The curving dunes are golden brown;
The shore-grass nods its slender head;
The hot white sand sifts slowly down,
Or slips beneath our hasty tread

Far runs the shore, a silver strand,
And skies meet seas in clouds of pearl;
The ocean's arms embrace the land,
And far aloft the swallows whirl.
Then lap, lap softly, on the shore,
Blue waters, lap! I rest and dream
Of ships that sail your surface o'er
And watch the shifting sunshine gleam.

Sail onward, ships! White wings, sail on,
Till past the horizon's purple bar
You drift from sight! In flush of dawn
Sail on, and, 'neath the evening star,
Fair skies be o'er you! Fair winds fill
Your swelling sails, till half the world
Be circled, and, in havens still,
Your weary wings be calmly furled.

Swoop, seagulls, swoop above the blue,
Nor fold till eve your pinions' snow!
Where sleep you, seagulls, when the dew
Dampens the sand and moons outglow?
Lap softly, purple waves! I dream,
And dreams are sweet. I'll wake no more,
But ever watch the white sails gleam,
And plovers flit along the shore!

When The Tide Goes Out

The boats sail out over murmurous seas,
  O'er reaches of dazzling blue,
Past islands like purple Hesperides
  Whence at dawn the sea-gulls flew;
Their white sails glisten in galaxies,
  When the tide goes out.

Afar, where the sky bends down to meet
  The ocean's pallid rim,
Drift fishing schooners — a shadowy fleet —
  Like phantom vessels dim
That never a shore or a landing greet,
  When the tide goes out.

The white sands glisten and burn and glow,
  And the rocky reefs are bare;
The great cloud argosies come and go
  In tranquil deeps of air;
The sea's own witchery we may know,
  When the tide goes out.

A calm has fallen o'er wave and shore —
  The calm of a coast of dreams —
And silver-pinioned sea-gulls soar
  Where the water pales and creams;
E'en the sorrowful ocean has hushed its roar,
  When the tide goes out.

Before Storm

There's a grayness over the harbor like fear on the face of a woman,
  The sob of the waves has a sound akin to a woman's cry,
And the deeps beyond the bar are moaning with evil presage
  Of a storm that will leap from its lair in that dour north-eastern sky.

Slowly the pale mists rise, like ghosts of the sea, in the offing,
  Creeping all wan and chilly by headland and sunken reef,
And a wind is wailing and keening like a lost thing 'mid the islands,
Boding of wreck and tempest, plaining of dolor and grief.

Swiftly the boats come homeward, over the grim bar crowding,
  Like birds that flee to their shelter in hurry and affright,
Only the wild gray gulls that love the cloud and the clamor
  Will dare to tempt the ways of the ravening sea to-night.

But the ship that sailed at the dawning, manned by the lads that love us
  God help and pity her when the storm is loosed on her track!
Oh women, we pray to-night and keep a vigil of sorrow
  For those we sped at the dawning and may never welcome back!

The Sandshore In September

Dim dusk on the sea where a star shines over —
The night steals across the sand,
Purply-brooding the shadows hover,
And by the headland a white-sail rover
Skims on to the darkening land.

Far in the west still the hue is glowing
Of a sunset's crimson death;
The troubled tide o'er the bar is flowing
And vibrant winds are coming and going
With the salt foam in their breath.

Slow from the eastward a fog is creeping,
Spectral and chill and white;
Soon it will wrap the wide sea sleeping,
And the sandshore, given o'er to its keeping,
Will dream and gleam through the night.

Why need we linger when o'er the meadows
The glow of our homelight shines?
Dear, let us leave the sandshore to its shadows
And hand in hand go across the meadows
To that love-star in the pines.

Part II
Poems of Humanity

Down Home

Down home to-night the moonshine falls
  Across a hill with daisies pied,
The pear-tree by the garden gate
  Beckons with white arms like a bride.

A savor as of trampled fern
  Along the whispering meadow stirs,
And, beacon of immortal love,
  A light is shining through the firs.

To my old gable-window creeps
  The night wind with a sigh and song,
And weaving ancient sorceries,
  Thereto the gleeful moonbeams throng.

Beside the open kitchen door
  My mother stands, all longingly,
And o'er the pathways of the dark
  She sends a yearning thought to me.

It seeks and finds my answering heart,
  Which shall no more be peace-possessed
Until I reach her empty arms
  And lay my head upon her breast.

Home From Town

There, I can draw a free breath!
I'm clear of the town once more, —
Clear of its dust and smoke, and deafening rattle and roar,
How anyone can live all his life in that place beats me!
One day's enough for my liking — and now I'm out and free.
Out in the country road where the air is sweet and dim,
And somewhere across the fields the frogs are singing a hymn;
And the moon is getting bright — she was pale 'fore the sun went
                                    down —
And in an hour wife'll say, "Your father's home from town,"
Hurry 'long smart now, Doll. Jack's waiting at the gate.
Listening for wheels, and wondering what's keeping me so late.
I've brought him a brand-new knife, with a corkscrew in it and all;
He's been coaxing for one ever since he broke his old one last fall.
How his eyes will shine! And then, there's the doll for May,
And the little work-box for Kate, and a couple of books for Ray,
— Always a-reading he is, cut out for a scholar, I guess.
Well, the boy shall have a chance. And here is the wife's new
                                    dress.
I got it for a surprise; she said her old one would do.
But I want to see her look nice — and this is a navy blue.
She's as pretty a woman still as I saw in town to-day.
And not one of the girls back there can hold a candle to May.
With her little golden curls, and pink on her dimpled face,
The prettiest flower that grows anywhere about the old place.
Jog along smarter, Doll — I can see the kitchen light
A-shining out through the trees — a particular pleasant sight;
And Jack's whistling at the gate; I can smell the clover hay,
— The boy must be tired if he mowed the big south meadow
                                    today,
And that little white thing there, a-standing close by his side?

It's my own little Mayflower, bless her! and of course she wants a
                                                           ride.
And Kate and Ray are coming as fast as they can down the lane,
And wife's at the kitchen door — I can see her just as plain!
What a look she'll give when I show her the brand-new merino
                                                          gown!
Down Rover, old dog — be careful. Well, I'm glad to be home
                                                    from town.

If I Were Home

If I were home on those dear green hills,
  In those wide and dewy meadows,
  Where the cattle pastured by lake and stream
  'Mid the ever-hurrying shadows;
Could I see once more the farmhouse old
  And the drowsy sunlight shining
Through door and casement where, pink with bloom,
  The roses are thickly twining,
I know full well that this weary pain
Would leave me and I should be free again
  From the fever's cruel fetter —
If only once more my longing eyes
Might look on the blue of the homeland skies,
  I know I should soon grow better.

If but once more I might drink the air
  Of the meadows brimmed with clover
And roam at will through the pastures wide
  Where rhythmic winds blow over;
Could I but hear in the still of the night
  The patter of raindrops falling,
The old-time croon of the poplar trees
  Or the cricket's harvest calling;
Could I see the dawn on those shadowy hills
Flame into the day while across the sills
  Its golden light came creeping
Then I know that my weary eyes would close
In the perfect rest of a calm repose
  A happy and painless sleeping.

Could I lie once more 'neath the orchard boughs
   Where I know my bees are humming,
And the whiffs of sweet old-fashioned flowers
   Are ever going and coming;
Could I stand at dusk in the darkling lane
   And hear the cowbells tinkle,
When the cows come home in the twilight dim
   And the stars are all a-twinkle;
Could I wander once more in my woodland nooks
And hear the call of my full-voiced brooks,
   How hope in my heart would flutter!
Oh, if I were home in the old-time calm
Of those quiet valleys their breathing balm
Would yield me from suffering a glad release
And fill my heart with a raptured peace
   Too deep for tongue to utter.

Interlude

To-day a wind of dream
  Blew down the raucous street . . .
I heard a hidden stream
  Laugh somewhere at my feet.

I felt a mist of rain
  Trembling against my face . . .
I knew that wind had lain
  In many a haunted place.

I saw a sea-beach dim
  By many a silver dune,
Where sandy hollows brim
  With magic of the moon.

I saw a shadowy ship
  Upon her seaward way,
And felt upon my lip
  A kiss of yesterday.

I walked again beside
  The dark enchantress Night
Until the dawn's white pride
  Brought back a lost delight.

O wind of dream, blow still,
  For I would have it stay . . .
That ghostly pressure sweet and chill,
  The kiss of yesterday.

Last Night In Dreams

Last night in dreams I went once more
   To my old home beside the sea;
I saw the sunrise on the shore,
   The harbor whitening mistily;
Oh, sweet it was to meet again
The morning coming up the glen!

I saw the uplands green and wide,
   The pines about the meadow spring,
The orchard with its shadows pied
   Where early robins waked to sing.
Oh, sweet once more to hear the trill
Of glad winds piping on the hill.

I saw my garden wet with dew,
   Where bloomed the flowers of long ago,
There red and white the roses grew
   And lilies lifted buds of snow;
Oh, sweet it was again to tread
Those ways with blossoms garlanded!

And when the happy day had gone
   Beyond the meadows far away,
I saw the twilight creeping on
   In vesper-hush of gold and gray;
Oh, sweet above the dim hill's crest
The first star sparkle in the west!

And when across the fragrant gloom
   A silver summer moonshine crept
I saw once more the gable room
   Where weary little children slept;
Oh, sweet beside its window there
To kneel again in childhood's prayer!

Oh, sweet my dream of morning seas,
  And sweet my dream of twilight star,
Sweet all those olden memories,
  But of them all the sweetest far
Was that once more I dropped to rest
With head upon a mother's breast.

Southernwood

What is it you have in the heart of your posy, stranger?
Well, well, if it isn't a sprig of southernwood!
From the country, I reckon? They call it out of the fashion,
But a whiff of its fragrance always does me good,
And to see a bit of it here in this grimy city street
'Minds me of home and mother and all things good and sweet.

It grew by the old front door in the homestead garden
Where we sat in the dusk at the time of stars and dew,
Just under the lilac-bush by the parlor window,
Where the breath of honeysuckle and clover meadows blew
    through,
With the orchards on either side in their fruitful solitude —
Oh, it all comes back to me now with the scent of southernwood!

Mother would have a sprig pinned always about her somewhere,
Or a bit to hold in her hand as she rested there at one side,
The roses and pinks were sweet, but she loved it better,
For she'd planted the roots herself when she came to the farm
    a bride.
And we tired boys and girls who sat at her feet
Felt only the time was dear and mother's face was sweet.

Now we're scattered far and away the wide world over —
When father and mother are gone the children are swift to roam!
The hillside farm has passed to the hands of others,
And strangers dwell in the spot we called our home,
But the garden old, and the house where the poplars stood,
Are mine again by the spell of the scent of southernwood.

The Apple-Picking Time

When September's purple asters stay to wreathe October's crown,
And the misty wooded hillslopes are red and golden brown,
When morns are hazy purple and wild geese eastward fly,
And fiery crimsons linger late along the evening sky,
When swallows on the barn roofs perch, to chatter of their flight,
When hints of frost are in the air, and crickets chirp at night,
Then come the pleasant days we love in autumn's mellow prime,
The jolliest days of all the year . . . the apple-picking time.
For the laden boughs are bending low o'er all the orchard ways,
The apples' cheeks are burning red, and father smiles and says,
Some sparkling morn, "I think to-day we might as well begin;
Be smart now boys! You'll need a week to get those apples in."

There are fresh young voices 'mong the trees and peals of
    laughter gay,
And the ruddy pile on the granary floor grows bigger every day,
While the tired old Earth a-napping lies in mellow magic light,
And there are tired hands and happy hearts in the old farmhouse
    at night:
For we pick from dawn till the autumn moon shines over the
    poplar hill,
And the stars peep down through the orchard boughs and the
    world is hushed and still.
And when the market apples have been carefully gathered in,
And every nook and corner's filled in granary, house and bin,
The best fun's still to come when in the orchard on the hill
We pick the cider apples and cart them to the mill.
What frolic and what shouting! Those apples need no care;
Just climb the trees and shake them down in pattering hundreds
    there.

It's fine down Winter's gleaming hills with arrow's speed to fly,
Or wade in some dusk woodland pool when Spring comes
    wandering by,
It's pleasant to listen in Summer hours to the breeze's wordless
    rhyme,
But it's jollier far just to be alive in the apple-picking time.

Coiling Up The Hay

There's many a thing we like to do, we boys upon the farm,
And every little duty has its own peculiar charm,
But I think we're most delighted when we hear our father say,
"A shower is coming up, I fear. Come, boys, and coil the hay."

The green and sweeping meadows lie wide open to the sun,
Where crickets chirp, and breezes blow, and frisky shadows run,
And the long, tangled, new-mown swaths are sweet with the
    perfume
That only comes from ripened grass and faded clover bloom.

Sometimes it's in the morning when the air is cool and sweet,
And sometimes in the afternoon beneath the sultry heat,
But oftener it's at twilight when the west is rosy red,
And big white stars are blinking out in tranquil deeps o'erhead.

With sturdy arms we toss the hay and shape the coils with care,
And merry voices echo through the golden evening air,
Till the last field is dotted o'er with haycocks neat and trim,
And the last lingering light has died across the uplands dim.

What care we now if summer showers fall in the coming night?
We've done our work with earnest care, and all is snug and tight.
We may be tired, but welcome rest will follow on the day,
And it's the jolliest sort of fun, this coiling up the hay.

The Gable Window

It opened on a world of wonder,
  When summer days were sweet and long,
A world of light, a world of splendor,
  A world of song.

'Twas there I passed my hours of dreaming,
  'Twas there I knelt at night to pray;
And, when the rose-lit dawn was streaming
  Across the day,

I bent from it to catch the glory
  Of all those radiant silver skies —
A resurrection allegory
  For human eyes!

The summer raindrops on it beating,
  The swallows clinging 'neath the eaves,
The wayward shadows by it fleeting,
  The whispering leaves;

The birds that passed in joyous vagrance,
  The echoes of the golden moon,
The drifting in of subtle fragrance,
  The wind's low croon;

Held each a message and a token
  In every hour of day and night;
A meaning wordless and unspoken,
  Yet read aright.

I looked from it o'er bloomy meadows,
  Where idle breezes lost their way,
To solemn hills, whose purple shadows
  About them lay.

I saw the sunshine stream in splendor
O'er heaven's utmost azure bars,
At eve the radiance, pure and tender,
Of white-browed stars.

I carried there my childish sorrows,
I wept my little griefs away;
I pictured there my glad to-morrows
In bright array.

The airy dreams of child and maiden
Hang round that gable window still,
As cling the vines, green and leaf-laden,
About the sill.

And though I lean no longer from it,
To gaze with loving reverent eyes,
On clouds and amethystine summit,
And star-sown skies.

The lessons at its casement taught me,
My life with rich fruition fill;
The rapture and the peace they brought me
Are with me still!

Grandmother's Garden

'Twas the dearest spot that my childhood knew,
That garden old where the roses grew
All pink and dewy with twinkling gems;
And lilies bent on their slender stems
To waft on the air their rich perfume
Blent with the breath of sweet clover bloom,
And the lilacs down by the sagging gate
In springtime days kept their purple state.

The light came down through the apple trees
That were pink with blossoms and gay with bees,
And lay in patches of golden sheen
The cool dim arches and aisles between;
While the cherry trees on the slope below
Were white as banks of December snow,
And along its border the poplars tall
Seemed like faithful guardians over all.

How we loved to loiter away the hours
In that fairy realm of light and flowers,
To chase each other among the trees
Where the fitful winds rang their symphonies,
Or dabble our feet where a shy brook stole
Across the corner below the knoll,
With a muffled call and a silvern gleam
That flashes still on my waking dream.

How we loved the scent of the southernwood
Where it grew in an emerald solitude
Beneath the lilacs, and dearer still
The honeysuckle around the sill
Of the old low windows and wide front door —
It all comes back to my sight once more;
And I seem to stand in the dear home place
Where the apple blossoms caress my face.

I hear the call of the hidden brook
And the robin's flute in each orchard nook,
I see the blue of the summer skies
And the dappled wings of the butterflies,
The silken poppies, the trim rose walks,
And the lilies a-nod on their slender stalks.
Once more the sweets of their breath I drain,
And a calm steals over my weary brain.

And grandmother comes to our resting place
With a loving smile on her dear old face,
As she did of old when the light grew dim
And the west was with sunset rose a-brim,
To call us away to our early rest
In the brown old cottage we loved the best;
And there we sink to a blessed sleep,
While over the garden the shadows creep.

In An Old Town Garden

Shut from the clamor of the street
  By an old wall with lichen grown,
It holds apart from the jar and fret
  A peace and beauty all its own.

The freshness of the springtime rains
  And dews of morning linger here;
It holds the glow of summer noons
  And ripest twilights of the year.

Above its bloom the evening stars
  Look down at closing of the day,
And in its sweet and shady walks
  Winds spent with roaming love to stray,

Upgathering to themselves the breath
  Of wide-blown roses white and red,
The spice of musk and lavender
  Along its winding alleys shed.

Outside our shadeless troubled streets
  And souls that quest for gold and gain,
Lips that have long forgot to smile
  And hearts that burn and ache with pain.

But here is all the sweet of dreams,
  The grace of prayer, the boon of rest;
The spirit of old songs and loves
  Dwells in this garden blossom-blest.

Here would I linger for a space,
  And walk herein with memory;
The world will pass me as it may
  And hope will minister to me.

The Light In Mother's Eyes

Dear beacon of my childhood's day,
  The lodestar of my youth,
A mingled glow of tenderest love,
  And firm unswerving truth,
I've wandered far o'er East and West,
  'Neath many stranger skies,
But ne'er I've seen a fairer light
  Than that in mother's eyes.

In childhood, when I crept to lay
  My tired head on her knee,
How gently shone the mother-love
  In those dear eyes on me,
And when in youth my eager feet
  Roamed from her side afar,
Where'er I went, that light divine
  Was aye my guiding star.

In hours when all life's sweetest buds
  Burst into dewy bloom;
In hours when cherished hopes lay dead,
  In sorrow and in gloom;
In evening's hush, or morning's glow,
  Or in the solemn night,
Those mother eyes still shed on me
  Their calm unchanging light.

Long since the patient hands I loved
  Were folded in the clay,
And long have seemed the lonely years,
  Since mother went away,
But still, I know she waits for me
  In fields of Paradise,
And I shall reach them yet, led by
  The light in mother's eyes.

An Old Face

Calm as a reaped harvest height
Lying in the dim moonlight,
Yet with wrinkles round the eyes,
Jolly, tolerant and wise;
Beauty gone but in its place
Such a savor, such a grace
Won from the fantastic strife
Of this odd business we call life.

Many a wild adventurous year
Wrote its splendid record here;
Stars of many an old romance
Shine in that ironic glance;
Many a hideous vital day
Came and smote and passed away;
Now this face is ripe and glad,
Patient, sane — a little sad.

Friend to life yet with no fear
Of the darkness drawing near;
These so gallant eyes must see
Dawn-light of eternity,
See the Secret Vision still
High on some supernal hill;
'Tis a daring hope I hold —
To look like this when I am old.

The Garden In Winter

Frosty, white and cold it lies
  Underneath the fretful skies;
Snowflakes flutter where the red
  Banners of the poppies spread;
And the drifts are wide and deep
  Where the lilies fell asleep.

But the sunsets o'er it throw
  Flame-like splendor, lucent glow,
And the moonshine makes it gleam
  Like a wonderland of dream;
And the sharp winds all the day
  Pipe and whistle shrilly gay.

Safe beneath the snowdrifts lie
  Rainbow buds of by-and-by,
In the long sweet days of spring,
  Music of bluebells will ring;
And its faintly golden cup
  Many a primrose will hold up.

Though the winds are keen and chill
  Roses' hearts are beating still,
And the garden tranquilly
  Dreams of happy hours to be;
In the summer days of blue
  All its dreamings will come true.

At The Dance

Rhythmic beating of dainty feet,
  Faces outvying the costly blooms,
Perfumes subtle, and strange and sweet;
  Music pulsing through brilliant rooms,
Sheen of satin, and foam of lace,
  Jewels a-glitter on arms of snow;
Girlish joy on each fair young face,
  Voices a-quiver and eyes aglow.

To-night, with the fairest girl I dance,
  Rumor has coupled our names, they say,
Eyes down-drooping beneath my glance;
  If I speak will she answer "Nay"?
Now in the waltz we smoothly whirl;
  Never was step than hers more light,
Why should the thought of another girl
  Come from a dance of the past to-night?

A harvest home of my boyhood's day,
  Little like this yet the fiddle's strain
Was witching — Old Amby knew how to play,
  To thrill with passion or stab with pain,
I danced with the belle; her eyes dropped down —
  Rumor had coupled our names, you see, —
Shy and sweet in her muslin gown;
  Fair and true as a girl need be.

Not a little like this one here —
  Hair very much the same bright hue —
Not so tall — pink of cheek as clear —
  Eyes, perchance, of a darker blue.
How we danced, with youth's own zest,
  Till the stars paled in the eastern sky,
And we two, with our love confessed,
  Walked home together, she and I.

Pardon, fair partner, of waltz and whirl,
  My errant dreams of a love untrue,
Was it treason to think of that other girl
  When my thoughts should only have been of you?
Come, I promise to dream no more,
  Look not up with reproachful glance,
Lightly drift we across the floor.
  I am yours, to-night at the dance.

Comparisons

Far in the gracious western sky
  Above the restless harbor bar,
A beacon on the coast of night,
  Shines out a calm, white evening star;
But your deep eyes, my 'longshore lass,
  Are brighter, clearer far.

The glory of the sunset past
  Still rests upon the water there;
But all its splendor cannot match
  The wind blown brightness of your hair;
Not any sea maid's floating locks
  Of gold are half as fair.

The waves are whispering to the sands
  With murmurs as of elfin glee;
But your low laughter, 'longshore lass,
  Is like a sea harp's melody,
And the vibrant tones of your tender voice
  Are sweeter far to me!

If Love Should Come

If love should come,
  I wonder if my restless troubled heart,
  Unkind, would bid its visitor depart,
    With chill averted look and pulse unthrilled,
    Because its sanctum was already filled
By cold ambition — would it still be dumb
    If love should come?

If love should come,
  Would all his pleading fall upon my ear
  Unrecked of, as by one who will not hear?
    Would my lips say, "I do not know thy name;
    I seek the far cold heights where dwelleth fame.
In all my life for thee there is no room."
    If love should come?

If love should come,
  Against him would I dare to bar the door,
  And, unregretful, bid him come no more?
    Would stern ambition whisper to my heart,
    "Love is a weakness — bid him hence depart,
For he and I can have no common home,"
    If love should come?

If love should come,
  And I should shut him out and turn away,
  Would what contents me now content me aye?
    Would all success the lonely years might bring
    Suffice to recompense for that one thing?
Ah, *could* my heart be silent, my lips dumb,
    If love should come?

In Lovers' Lane

I know a place for lagging feet
  Deep in the valley where the breeze
Makes melody in lichened boughs
  And murmurs low love-litanies.

There slender harebells nod and dream,
  And pale wild-roses offer up
The fragrance of their golden hearts
  As from some incense-brimmed cup.

It holds the sunshine sifted down
  Softly through many a beechen screen,
Save where by deeper woods embraced
  Cool shadows linger dim and green.

And there my love and I may walk
  And harken to the lapsing fall
Of unseen brooks, and tender winds,
  And wooing birds that sweetly call.

And every voice to her will say
  What I repeat in dear refrain,
And eyes will meet with seeking eyes
  And hands will clasp in Lovers' Lane.

Come, sweetheart, then, and we will stray
  Adown that valley, lingering long
Until the rose is wet with dew
  And robins come to even-song;

And woo each other, borrowing speech
  Of love from winds and brooks and birds
Until our sundered thoughts are one
  And hearts have no more need of words.

The Bride Dreams

Love, is it dawn that creeps in so gray,
Like the timid ghost,
All shrinking and pale, of the sweet dead night
Lived and enjoyed to the uttermost
Of its swift delight?
Love, hold me close, for I am a-cold
With the grave's own chill,
And my cheek must yet have the smear of the mould —
I have dreamed a dream as here I lay
Next to your heart —in my dream I died
And was buried deep, deep in the yard beside
The old church on the hill.
(Oh, the dream was bitter!)

II

By my gravestone a rose was blowing red,
Red as my love,
The world was full of the laughter of spring —
I heard it down there in my clammy bed —
The little birds sang in the trees above,
The wind was glad with the clouds that fled
All white and pearly across the sky,
And the pretty shadows went winking by
Like tricksy madcap thoughts a-wing.

You had buried me in my wedding gown
Of silk and lace —
My hair curled blackly my neck adown,
But my lips, I knew, were white in my face,
And the flower I held in my stiff hand yet
Was slimy and wet.
(Keep me from death, oh, my lover!)

III

Still, though the clay was heaped over me,
I could see — I could see
The folk going by to the old church door;
Wives and mothers and maids went by
All fine and silken, rosy and sweet;
Some came with a tear their graves to greet,
But to mine only old mad Margaret came,
And she laughed to herself as she read my name
With an eerie laughter, evil and sly,
That pierced like a dart to my cold heart's core.

I saw the old maid go bitterly in
Who had known no love —
Two brothers who hated each other well —
Miser Jock with his yellow skin —
A girl with the innocent eyes of a dove —
A young wife with a bonny child —
And Lawrence, the man who never smiled
With his lips, but always mocked with his eyes —
O love, the grave makes far too wise,
(I knew why he mocked!)

IV

Then I felt a thrill the dank earth through
And I knew — Oh, I knew
That it came from your step on our path from the dale;
Almost my heart began to beat!
Proud of her golden ring, at your side —
That slim white girl who lives at the mill,
Who has loved you always and loves you still,
With her hair the color of harvest wheat
And her lips as red as mine were pale.

How I hated her, so tall and fair
And shining of hair —
Love, I am so little and dark!
My heart, that had once soared up like a lark
At your glance, was as a stone in my breast;
Never once did you look my way,
Only at *her* you looked and kissed
With your eyes her eyes of amethyst —
My eyes were sunk in cruel decay
And the worms crawled in the silk of my vest —
(Keep me from death, Oh, my lover!)

V

Love, hold me close for I am a-cold!
It was only a dream — as a dream it fled,
Kiss me warm from its lingering chill,
Burn from my face the taint of the dead,
Kiss my hair that is black not gold —
Am I not sweet as the girl at the mill?
(Oh, the dream was bitter!)

My Legacy

My friend has gone away from me,
  From shadow into perfect light,
But leaving a sweet legacy.

My heart shall hold it long in fee —
  A grand ideal calm and bright,
A song of hope for ministry,

A faith of unstained purity,
  A thought of beauty for delight —
These did my friend bequeath to me;

And more than even these can be,
  The worthy pattern of a white
Unmarred life lived most graciously.

Dear comrade, loyal thanks to thee
  Who now hath fared beyond my sight,
My friend has gone away from me,
But leaving a sweet legacy.

The Parting Soul

Open the casement and set wide the door
  For one out-going
Into the night that slips along the shore
  Like a dark river flowing;
The rhythmic anguish of our sad hearts' beating
Must hinder not a soul that would be fleeting.

Hark, how the voices of the ghostly wind
  Cry for her coming!
What wild adventurous playmates will she find
  When she goes roaming
Over the starry moor and misty hollow?
Loosen the clasp and set her free to follow.

Open the casement and set wide the door —
  The call is clearer!
Than we whom she has loved so well before
  There is a dearer —
When her fond lover death for her is sighing
We must not hold her with our tears from dying.

With Tears They Buried
You Today

With tears they buried you to-day,
  But well I knew no turf could hold
  Your gladness long beneath the mould,
Or cramp your laughter in the clay;
I smiled while others wept for you,
Because I knew.

And now you sit with me to-night,
  Here in our old accustomed place;
  Tender and mirthful is your face;
Your eyes with starry joy are bright.
Oh, you are merry as a song,
For love is strong!

They think of you as lying there,
  Down in the churchyard grim and old;
  They think of you as mute and cold,
A wan white thing that once was fair,
With dim sealed eyes that never may
Look on the day.

But love cannot be coffined so
  In cold and darkness; it must rise
  And seek its own in radiant guise,
With immortality aglow,
Making of death's triumphant sting
A little thing.

Ay, we shall laugh at those who deem
   Our hearts are sundered! Listen, sweet;
   The tripping of the wind's swift feet,
Along the byways of our dream,
And hark the whisper of the rose
Wilding that blows.

Oh, still you love those simple things,
   And still you love them more with me;
   The grave has won no victory;
It could not clasp your shining wings;
It could not keep you from my side,
Dear and my bride!

I Asked Of God

Humbly I asked of God to give me joy,
  To crown my life with blossoms of delight;
I pled for happiness without alloy,
  Desiring that my pathway should be bright;
Prayerful I sought these blessings to attain, —
  And now I thank him that he gave me pain.

I asked of God that he should give success
  To the high task I sought for him to do;
I asked that all the hindrances grow less,
  And that my hours of weakness might be few;
I asked that far and lofty heights be scaled, —
  And now I meekly thank him that I failed.

For with the pain and sorrow came to me
  A dower of tenderness in act and thought;
And with the failure came a sympathy,
  An insight that success had never bought.
Father, I had been foolish and unblest
  If thou had granted me my blind request!

A Thanksgiving

Father, I thank Thee that I saw tonight
The moonrise on the sea;
I thank Thee for the blossoms frosty-white
Outflowering on the lea;
I thank Thee for the silence consecrate
In vast cathedral woods;
I thank Thee for the winds that soon and late
Pipe in far solitudes.

I thank Thee for a word that came to me
A friend's heart to express;
I thank Thee for an old grief grown to be
A thing of helpfulness;
I thank Thee for the task that I must do
Lacking in lavish ease,
For a dear hope, for an ideal true —
Father, all thanks for these!

We Have Seen His Star

Across the yellow, pathless desert sands,
  And over mountains in the East afar,
We come with royal tribute in our hands,
  For we have seen his star;
We seek the New-born, we the ancient kings,
  Hoary in lore of Persian and Chaldee,
  Because immortal life, rich, full and free,
This Baby with Him brings.

Old, very old, are we, and we have sought
  The Greater Knowledge, lo! these many years;
Yearned for the truth and ever found it not,
  For all our toil and tears.
But He is truth incarnate; at His feet
  When we shall kneel in homage reverently,
  The wisdom we have quested for shall be
Ours grandly and complete.

Long have we blindly groped our stumbling road,
  Seeking the light, though wandering oft astray,
But now the path shall be made plain to God —
  He comes to show the way;
Long hath our journey been from lands afar,
  Costly and splendid are the gifts we bring,
  Tell us, we pray thee now, where lies the King,
For we have seen His star.

The Choice

Life, come to me in no pale guise and ashen,
I care not for thee in such placid fashion!
  I would share widely, Life,
  In all thy joy and strife,
Would sound thy deeps and reach thy highest passion,
With thy delight and with thy suffering rife.

Whether I bide with thee in cot or palace,
I would drink deeply, Life, of thy great chalice,
  Even to its bitter lees, —
  Yea, shrinking not from these,
Since out of bitterness come strength and solace,
And wisdom is not won in slumberous ease.

Wan peace, uncolored days, were a poor favor;
To lack great pain and love were to lack savor.
  Life, take the heart of me
  And fill it brimmingly,
No matter with what poignant brew or flavor,
So that it may not shrunk and empty be.

Yea, Life, thus would I live, nor play at living,
The best of me for thy best gladly giving,
  With an unfaltering cheer
  Greeting thee year by year,
Even in thy dourest mood some good achieving,
Until I read thy deep-hid meaning clear!

Could We But Know

Could we but know how often worn and weary
  Are those we meet;
Would we condemn because they call life bitter,
  Which we think sweet?
Would not our thought and judgment be more tender
  To friend and foe,
Our greeting warmed with more of love's own kindness,
  Could we but know?

Could we but know how pain may lurk 'neath laughter —
  Too keen to bear —
And how the hearts we deem so hard and reckless
  Are dark with care,
Would not our idle tongues be slow to utter
  Our words of blame?
Would we not call what we had reckoned folly
  Some gentler name?

Would we not think 'twere wise to be forgiving
  Of doubtful mood,
Of all mistakes and seeming slights and errors
  Not understood?
Would not our feet be swifter in the going
  Help to bestow?
Our own lives better, nobler for the knowing,
  Could we but know?

I Wish You

Friend o' mine, in the year oncoming
I wish you a little time for play,
And an hour to dream in the eerie gloaming
After the clamorous day.
(And the moon like a pearl from an Indian shore
To hang for a lantern above your door.)

A little house with friendly rafters,
And some one in it to need you there,
Wine of romance and wholesome laughters
With a comrade or two to share.
(And some secret spot of your very own
Whenever you want to cry alone.)

I wish you a garden on fire with roses,
Columbines planted for your delight,
Scent of mint in its shadowy closes,
Clean, gay winds at night.
(Some nights for sleeping and some to ride
With the broomstick witches far and wide.)

A goodly crop of figs to gather,
With a thistle or two to prick and sting;
Since a harvesting too harmless is rather
An unadventurous thing.
(And now and then, spite of reason or rule,
The chance to be a bit of a fool.)

I wish you a thirst that can never be sated
For all the loveliness earth can yield,
Slim, cool birches whitely mated,
Dawn on an April field.
(And never too big a bill to pay
When the Fiddler finds he must up and away.)

The Land Of Some Day

Across the river of By-and-By,
  That is bridged by Dreams, they say,
Is a wonderful, beautiful, mystic land
  And this realm is named Some Day.

And everything fair in that country is,
  And pleasant to ear and eye.
And it doesn't really seem hard to cross
  The river of By-and-By.

The fame that we mean to win is there,
  The success for which we yearn,
There the friends await us, we hope to make,
  And the fortunes we hope to earn.

The books we'll write or the songs we'll sing,
  Or the power we intend to sway;
All the wonderful things that we mean to do
  Are found in this fair Some Day.

And everyone sometimes intends to reach
  That land that looks so near,
But somehow it seems to drift farther off
  With every succeeding year.

Some never contrive to make a start,
  In spite of all they've planned;
And others have striven but never reached
  That misty alluring strand.

Some fell through Dreams into By-and-By,
  And others lost their way
And wandered many a weary step,
  But never reached Some Day.

Oh, then beware of that treacherous shore,
   Though it seems so fair to view,
For I've heard it whispered that pleasant land
   Is but a mirage untrue.

And that no matter how long we search,
   It will seem just as far away,
For nobody ever yet was known
   Who really reached Some Day.

The Only Way

To chisel a statue unerringly
From the formless marble to symmetry,
How firm must the hand of the sculptor be!
Deep in his brain must he shape the thought
Ere in loveliness of stone it be wrought,
Hard must he toil at his great design,
Ere the work be perfect in curve and line.

To paint a picture that holds in fee
The treasure of beauty's alchemy,
How skilful the hand of the artist must be!
Ere the vast conception that burst to bloom
In his soul on the canvas fair finds room,
Many and long are the patient days
He must give to his task to win its praise.

To shape a life into harmony
With God's plans for it, gracious and free,
How true must the hand of the workman be!
Not in a day may the task be done,
Not with ease may success be won.
Hard must we work and aspire and pray —
Earnest toil is the only way!

The Revelation

Once to my side a veilèd figure came
  To bear me company.
Deeming that Sorrow was her bitter name,
  I strove from her to flee.
She clasped my hand in hers and led me on
  Beneath a clouded sky;
Till many dour and dreary days had gone,
  Right sullenly went I.

But as time passed I grew to love my guide,
  No more escape I sought;
At last contented by her gentle side
  To learn the lessons taught.
Then lifted she her veil and showed to me
  Her calm eternal youth.
"Lo! Mortal, who has known my ministry,
  Behold me — I am Truth."

A Smile

What is a smile? A sudden gleam
  Of sunshine welling in the eyes,
  That quickly comes and quickly flies,
The outlet of some radiant dream?
Well, then a smile's a blithesome thing
  Whose pure delight and painless birth
  Might bear to every soul on earth
The gladness of its hidden spring.

What is a smile? A glint of scorn
  At some poor soul's mistake or fear,
  The keen refinement of a sneer
From secret hate or malice born?
Nay, then a smile's a hateful thing
  And bears a sharp unpitying dart
  To many a wearied aching heart,
To linger there and wound and sting.

What is a smile? The gentle glow
  Upon the edges of a tear,
  To chastened grief and sorrow near,
Yet with a blessing to bestow?
Ah, then a smile's a holy thing
  From a tired spirit's victory sent
  To whisper hope and courage blent
To all the weak and suffering.

What is a smile? A treacherous screen
 To lure unwary, heedless feet,
 And mask the workings of deceit
Behind its beauty all unseen?
Nay, then a smile's a loathsome thing
 That carries in its gleam a blight
 To murder joy and kill delight,
And over life a shadow fling.

What is a smile? A shy glad burst
 Of love in true and timid eyes,
 Bewildered with the sweet surprise
Of tenderness in secret nurst?
Ah, then a smile's a glorious thing,
 Love's own inspired oracle
 To say what words can never tell,
And thrill each heart's responsive string.

Success

Come, drain the cup held to our lips at last,
Though it may yield the briny taste of tears,
For this we have forgone our joy of youth,
For this we have lived bitter, patient years . . .
What tang does brew of fig and thistle keep?
Let us drink deep!

Oh, shudder not . . . the goblet is of gold!
For this we bent our knee at a grim shrine
While others danced to kind and merry gods,
For this we put aside life's choicest wine . . .
To slake our still unsated thirst lift up
This sacramental cup.

Surely 'twill pay for all that we have missed . . .
Laughter unlaughed, sweet hours of love and sleep,
Hungers unsatisfied and barren dreams . . .
How the sly years are mocking us! Drink deep
And vaunt . . . for who can guess it is a lie? . . .
The price was not too high.

Was it for such a devil's jorum we
Bartered our precious things and turned from ease,
Winning by dint of many a gallant day
Splendid defeats and abject victories?
But see you now how bright the diamonds wink?
Be brave . . . once more . . . and drink!

The Test

All the great house sat hushed and listening
  There 'neath the music's spell,
Laughter and tears in bright eyes were glistening
  When the painted curtain fell;
Thunderous applause uprose to greet,
  I was their darling then.
Incense and homage at my feet
  They poured, those women and men!

Think you then that my heart was flattered,
  Dream I was satisfied?
Praise or censure, it nothing mattered
  When I had glanced aside;
There in the shadows across my right
  Sat the Artist, old and grey,
Never a motion made he that night
  To approve or applaud my play!

Silent he sat when the house was cheering
  — Bitter that hour to me!
What cared I for the fickle veering
  Of fancy's wind? It was he,
He, the master, I strove to please.
  Naught had my hope availed,
That grim old veteran of victories
  Was silent . . . I had failed.

The Two Guests

Came on a time two guests to me
    Named of the angels Joy and Sorrow
Said, "We seek to sojourn with thee,
    One to-day and one to-morrow.
Wisdom both in our hands we hold
    That cannot be bought by toil or gold.
Choose then which shall be first to stay,"
    "Joy," I cried, "be my guest to-day."

Joy came in and abode with me,
    Taught me much of the hearts around me,
The meaning of all glad things that be,
    Left me wiser than she had found me,
Passed from my door at set of sun,
    Saying, "With thee my work is done."
Thought I, grieving to lose my guest,
    Joy of all teachers is wisest and best.

Then took Sorrow my empty heart,
    Filled it up with her brewage bitter,
Deep I drank to my pain and smart,
    Face to face with that gloomy sitter
Lo! From my eyes there fell away
    Mists that had dimmed them till that day.
Rightly read I then human strife,
    Saw far down to the deeps of life.

Saw, and knew that Joy had not
To me such clearness of vision given,
For the barriers between thought and thought
By Sorrow's hand might alone be riven.
Costly the price that my soul must pay
But the boon so purchased was mine for aye!
Thought I, loving at last my guest,
"Sorrow of teachers is wisest and best."

The Words I Did Not Say

Many a word my tongue has uttered
  Has brought me sorrow at eventide,
And I have grieved with a grieving bitter
  Over speech of anger and scorn and pride,
But never a word in my heart remembered
  As I sit with myself at the close of day,
Has pierced with repentance more unavailing
  Than have the words I did not say.

The word of cheer that I might have whispered
  To a heart that was breaking with weight of woe,
The word of hope that I might have given
  To one whose courage was ebbing low,
The word of warning I should have spoken
  In the ear of one who walked astray.
Oh, how they come with a sad rebuking
  Those helpful words that I did not say;

So many and sweet: If I had but said them
  How glad my heart then would have been;
What a dew of blessing would fall upon it
  As the day's remembrances gather in;
But I said them not and the chance forever
  Is gone with the moments of yesterday,
And I sit alone with a spirit burdened
  By all the words that I did not say.

The morrow will come with its new beginning,
  Glad and grand, through the morning's gates —
Shall I not then with this thought beside me
  Go bravely forth to the work that waits?
Giving a message of cheer and kindness
  To all I meet on the world's highway,
So that I never will grieve at twilight
  Over the words that I did not say.

Which Has More Patience — Man Or Woman?

As my letter must be brief,
I'll at once state my belief,
And this it is — that, since the world began,
And Adam first did say,
"'Twas Eve led me astray,"
A woman hath more patience than a man.

If a man's obliged to wait
For some one who's rather late,
No mortal ever got in such a stew,
And if something can't be found
That he's sure should be around,
The listening air sometimes grows fairly blue.

Just watch a man who tries
To soothe a baby's cries,
Or put a stove pipe up in weather cold,
Into what a state he'll get;
How he'll fuss and fume and fret
And stamp and bluster round and storm and scold!

Some point to Job with pride,
As an argument for their side!
Why, it was so rare a patient man to see,
That when one was really found,
His discoverers were bound
To preserve for him a place in history!

And while I admit it's true
That man has some patience too,
And that woman isn't always sweetly calm,
Still I think all must agree
On this central fact — that she
For general all-round patience bears the palm.

All Aboard For Dreamland

The stars are a-wink in the drowsy skies.
The shadows are softly creeping down
Alas and alack for the sleepy eyes!
It's time for the ferry to Dreamland Town.

Here are the passengers one and all
The fare is a kiss and away we go
Never an accident may befall
For mother is captain and crew you know.

Away and away from the daytime shore
To a lullaby song we are drifting down
With a sail of moonshine and silver oar
In a poppy shallop to Dreamland Town.

Past the realms of elf and fay
And the caves of giants on either hand
Never a moment may we stay
In even the wonderful Brownie Land.

Captain, sing but a minute more
For the eyes of blue and the eyes of brown
Then the fare is paid and the trip is o'er
And here we are safely in Dreamland Town.

The Grumble Family

There's a family nobody likes to meet,
They live, it is said, on Complaining Street,
In the city of Never-are-Satisfied,
The river of Discontent beside.
They growl at that and they growl at this,
Whatever comes there is something amiss:
And whether their station be high or humble
They all are known by the name of Grumble.

The weather is always too hot or cold,
Summer and winter alike they scold;
Nothing goes right with the folks you meet
Down on that gloomy Complaining Street.
They growl at the rain and they growl at the sun,
In fact their growling is never done.
And if everything pleased them, there isn't a doubt
They'd growl that they'd nothing to grumble about.

But the queerest thing is that not one of the same
Can be brought to acknowledge his family name,
For never a Grumbler will own that he
Is connected with it at all, you see.
And the worst thing is that if any one stays
Among them too long he will learn their ways,
And before he dreams of the terrible jumble
He's adopted into the family of Grumble.

So it were wisest to keep our feet
From wandering into Complaining Street;
And never to growl whatever we do
Lest we be mistaken for Grumblers too.
Let us learn to walk with a smile and song,
No matter if things do sometimes go wrong,
And then, be our station high or humble,
We'll never belong to the family of Grumble.

In Twilight Land

In twilight land there are beautiful things —
The soft low songs that a mother sings,
Good-night kisses so fond and sweet,
Patters and twinkles of dimpled feet,
And the brightness of dreams that come sliding down
On a starry stairway from Slumbertown.

In twilight land where the shadows creep
Dear little eyes fall fast asleep,
Birds and blossoms have gone to rest
And babies are cuddled to mother's breast,
And always are tenderly whispered there
The sacred words of the children's prayer.

The Quest Of Lazy-Lad

Have you heard the tale of Lazy-Lad
  Who dearly loved to shirk,
For he "hated" his lessons and "hated" his tasks,
  And he "hated" to have to work?
So he sailed away on a summer day
  Over the ocean blue;
Said Lazy-Lad, "I will seek till I find
  The Land of Nothing-to-do.

For that is a jolly land I know,
  With never a lesson to learn,
And never an errand to bother a fellow
  Till he doesn't know where to turn.
And I'm told the folks in that splendid place
  May frolic the whole year through,
So everybody good-by — I'm off
  For the Land of Nothing-to-do!"

So Lazy-Lad he sailed to the west
  And then to the east sailed he,
And he sailed north and he sailed south
  Over many a league of sea,
And many a country fair and bright
  And busy came into view;
But never, alas, could he find the coast
  Of the Land of Nothing-to-do.

Then Lazy-Lad sailed back again,
   And a wiser lad was he,
For he said, "I've wandered to every land
   That is in the geography,
And in each and all I've found that folks
   Are busy the whole year through,
And everybody in every place
   Seemed to have something to do.

So it must be the best way after all
   And I mean to stay on shore
And learn my lessons and do my tasks
   And be Lazy-Lad no more.
The busiest folks are the happiest,
   And what mother said was true,
For I've found out there is no such place
   As the Land of Nothing-to-do."

Up In The Poplars

Up in the poplars all together
Five of us swung in the blithesome weather,
Long ago in the garden old,
When the sunshine fell in showers of gold
Through a leafy riot of dancing shadows.
And over and up from the clover meadows
Winds blew dreamily, odor-freighted,
From hills that ever in calmness waited.
There in the poplars we were sitting,
Golden visions around us flitting.
Three of us lads with the fire of youth,
And two were girls with eyes of truth.
All of us dreamers all together,
There in the mellow summer weather.

Nell, with her dark eyes' flashing splendor,
Lil, with her sweet voice, low and tender,
Dick and Tom, with their laughter gay —
All of us light at heart that day.
There we talked of the years on-coming,
Heart and fancy alike went roaming,
Nell was a singer laurel-crowned,
Known and praised all the world around;
Lil, a nurse on the field of battle,
Angel-faced 'mid the roar and rattle;

Dick was a sailor to far-off seas
And islands as fair as Hesperides.
Tom was an artist with brush inspired,
I was a writer with pen untired —
All of us famous there together
Up in the poplars in summer weather.

Up in the poplars we swung and chattered —
What were our dreamings little mattered.
Wealth and fame we were sure of winning,
There in the joyance of life's beginning —
Never a thought of the world's sure sorrow,
Never a fear of the dim tomorrow.
Alas, for the dreams we dreamed together
There in the heartsome summer weather!

Dark-eyed Nellie is soundly sleeping
Where far-off mountains their watch are keeping.
Lil in a humble home is queen.
Tom is a merchant, hard and keen.
And Dick, the careless and debonair,
Is a gouty, unhappy millionaire,
While I am a penniless, unknown rover
Hither and thither, the wide world over.
Alas for the dreams we dreamed together
Up in the poplars in summer weather.

What Children Know

Many things the children know —
Where the ripest berries grow,
Where the first pale violets peep
Shyly from their winter's sleep,
And how many blue eggs rest
In the robin's woven nest.

Children know where echoes hide
Over on the brown hillside,
How to tell a fortune bright
By the daisy petals white,
How the honey you may sup
From the meadow clover's cup.

Something else the children know —
Oh, they learned it long ago!
Mother's shoulder is the best
Place in all the world to rest.
And the sweetest dreams belong
To a mother's twilight song!

The New Year's Book

The book of the New Year lies open to you,
Dear lassies and lads, to be all written through.
Its pages have never a spot or a stain:
See to it that unspoiled and unmarred they remain,
  Taking all care,
  With effort and prayer,
To make of this volume a thing pure and fair.

Write in it no record of wrong and of ill
But kindness and courage and deeds of good will.
Let nothing of evil creep stealthily in
To darken the pages with shadows of sin,
    But write every day,
    As the year goes its way,
Shining thoughts of high worth that will sparkle for aye.

Put in it the splendor and hope of your youth,
Lines of honor and glory and beauty and truth,
Temptations o'ermastered and weakness made strong,
The sunshine of smiles and the blessing of song,
    Striving always that not
    A mistake or a blot
This beautiful book of the year may bespot.

For this record once written is written for aye,
No time can erase, no repentance gainsay,
With its evil or good, with its joy and its tears,
It is signed and sealed fast by the angel of years.
    Then let us take heed,
    Since God hath decreed
In eternity's halls what we've written we'll read.

Farewell

Sunset: and all the distant hills are shrouded
  In dusky golden light!
Day burns herself to death in funeral splendor
  Before the birth of night.

I stand beside the softly flowing river
  Its deeps another sky,
Far up the winding curves are lost in glory
  Far down the shadows lie.

Across the prairie misty glooms are creeping
  And clustering by the stream;
The evening breezes rustle mid the branches
  And all things lonely seem.

Half-sad, I gaze upon the noble river
  In its remorseless flow;
Onward and onward ever — all regardless
  Of human joy or woe.

A dewy hush; I hear the softened chiming
  Of some faint, far-off bell;
And here beneath the golden skies of sunset,
  I come to say — farewell!

Proud river, rolling past the floods of ages;
  Fair isles with beauty crowned!
Dark forests tossing weirdly 'gainst the golden
  Dim misty hills beyond.

'Tis time to bid farewell to these and hasten
  To a far distant land,
Back where the ocean moans in ceaseless sorrow
  On the Atlantic's strand.

Farewell! blue tide of mighty waters
 A living friend you seem;
How oft in rapture gazing on your beauty,
 I've wandered by your stream.

Your spirit speaks to mine in nature's music
 Beneath the darkening light;
'Tis with a saddened heart — that now I bid thee
 A long farewell to-night.

Farewell, ye prairies, bright in sunlit beauty
 Where buds of sweetness bloom,
Where breezes float across the dimpled lakelets
 In breaths of rich perfume.

Bright pleasant memories round your hillsides cluster
 And through the coming years
Your fairy slopes my thoughts will oft revisit
 Farewell, with many tears.

Farewell dark forests with your lonely vistas,
 Your secrets of the past,
The mystic whisper of your soughing branches
 Your purple shadows cast!

Your myriad voices answer through the stillness
 In one long shivering sigh:
Farewell, farewell, they seem to whisper softly
 And then in silence die.

Farewell, dear friends, your kindness I will cherish
 Among all memories sweet
Long years may pass ere once again I'll greet you,
 Yet oft in thought we'll meet.

Farewell, Prince Albert, pride of western prairies!
  Bright may thy future be;
Rise to a noble and a wealthy city,
  Farewell, farewell to thee.

Fainter and fainter grow the distant outlines
  And phantom shadows glide
Where 'neath the thickets of o'erhanging branches
  Plashes the rippling tide.

In the far blue some early stars are shining,
  The west has lost its light
All sounds are mingled in one gentle murmur
  Beneath the touch of night.

I turn to go "my eyes with tears are misty"
  Still rings that distant bell
Hills, prairies, forests, river, all — I bid you
  One last, one long farewell.

On Cape Le Force

(A legend of the early days of Prince Edward Island)

One evening, when the sun was low,
  I stood upon the wave-kissed strand,
And watched the white-sailed boats glide by,
  Their sails by evening breezes fanned.

In dimpling azure lay the sea,
  The rippling wavelets tinged with gold,
While to the rosy-clouded west
  A sparkling path of glory rolled.

I climbed the rocky cliffs and gained
  A rugged cape, around whose sides
The wavelets crept with moaning sigh,
  Or surges dashed their mighty tides.

Behind the lovely village lay
  The fertile fields of waving green,
Fair sloping hills and quiet dales,
  With spruce and maple groves between.

Before me slept that peerless sea,
  Its beauty tranquil and serene:
Search all our lovely Island o'er
  Thou wilt not find a fairer scene.

I stood upon that lovely cliff
  And called to mind the legend dread
Which made it an accursed spot —
  One shunned by superstitious tread.

'Twas years ago — ere yet the flag
  Of Britain claimed our loyalty,
And fair Prince Edward Island owned
  Allegiance to the fleur-de-lis.

When war's dark cloud hung threatening low
   Above our fair Canadian land,
And echoes of the troubled strife
   Reached e'en our Island's quiet strand;

And o'er our blue Saint Lawrence Gulf
   Sailed many a plundering privateer,
Defying law and right and force
   In their piratical career.

But, when the strife of war had passed
   And gentle Peace resumed her reign,
They met the fate they well deserved —
   Captured or wrecked upon the main.

And one — a treasure-laden ship —
   Was stranded here one autumn day,
And off this headland, lone and bleak,
   With all her precious freight she lay;

And, loth to lose his ill-won wealth,
   The captain planned how he might save
The treasure that his vessel held
   From English foes or ocean wave.

"The shore," he said, "is bleak and wild,
   The rocks no human footsteps bear;
And death will seal the lips of those
   Who know I hide the treasure there."

So all that sunny autumn day,
   The captain and his pirate band
Bore untold wealth from ship to shore
   And hid it on the rocky strand.

But, when the western sky had pealed
   And darkness veiled the forests wide,
They tented on the lonely cape
   To wait the dawn of morning tide.

Then rose the bursts of laughter wild,
    Mingled with curses deep and strong,
The taunting sneer, the fierce reply,
    The vulgar joke, and drunken song.

Wild was the scene; but when the moon
    Rose slowly up the eastern blue,
Tipping the dark fir trees with light,
    Unconscious lay the drunken crew.

And all were wrapped in heavy sleep
    Save two — the captain and the mate —
Who sat together in a tent,
    Their faces drawn with rage and hate.

And, as they sat, above them poised
    The friends of hatred and despair,
Of malice, envy, murder, scorn,
    Revenge and avarice — all were there.

There, to divide their ill-won gains
    And plan the murder of the crew,
Had met those different types of crime,
    And quarrelled — as all such will do.

Facing each other, there they sat —
    The captain, tall and dark and stern,
With sneering lip and glittering eye,
    Where all dark passions seemed to burn.

The mate, with vicious brutal face,
    Growled, like some snarling beast at bay
Defiant threats and savage oaths
    Of vengeance on the coming day.

"Well, be it so," the captain cried,
    "To-morrow, when the sun shall rise,
Our pistols will decide our claims
    And one shall lose or win the prize.

Good night, my friend, and pleasant dreams,
    I leave you now till dawn of day."
He bowed with air of mocking scorn
    And sought the moonlight's silver ray.

The night was calm; all sounds were hushed,
    Save for some lonely night-bird's cry,
Or wavelets splashing on the shore,
    Or cool night-breezes rustling by.

All night, upon the sullen verge,
    With restless tread the captain walked,
While o'er the sea the moonbeams played
    And shadows past the headland stalked.

Did some presentiment of ill,
    Upon the morrow, cross his brain?
Felt he repentance for the past?
    Or schemed he but fresh crimes again?

At length, when morning flushed the east,
    The rivals met. The half-drunk crew
Stood huddled in a powerless group,
    Not knowing what to say or do.

A look of craven fear was stamped
    Upon the mate's low, brutal face,
Mingled with sinister cunning, as
    Before the tent he took his place.

The captain, calm, composed and firm,
    Betrayed no trace of doubt or fear;
His face still wore its cool contempt,
    His lips, their cold sardonic sneer.

"Twelve paces off, I'll stand," he said,
    And, with his pistol in his hand,
He lightly turned upon his heel
    And calmly walked toward his stand.

Sudden the mate his pistol raised —
What need is there the rest to tell?
A sharp report! and, in his blood,
Shot through the heart, the captain fell.

Then 'ere the fear-struck crew could stir,
Flinging his weapon from his hand,
The guilty wretch sprang down the cliff
And fled along the rocky strand.

No hand was raised to stay his flight;
Few knew the crime, nor cared who did,
And 'ere the sun had left the wave,
The murderer was in safety hid.

And ne'er was he to justice brought,
For, in those days of blood and strife,
Murder was deemed a light offence
And lightly held was one man's life.

And, on this lonely wind-swept cape
Right where the murdered captain fell,
A hasty grave the sailors made,
And winds and surges rang his knell.

Forgotten in his lonely grave
He slept, while years unnumbered fled,
And dark traditions of the spot
Enwrapped it with unfading dread.

. . . . .

Long since, all vestige of the grave
Has vanished — but the legend lives,
And to this headland's rocky steeps
A weird and awful interest gives.

And, to this day, this lonely cape,
Which stems the billows stormy course,
Still bears the name of him who fell
Upon its summit — Cape Le Force.

June!

"Wake up," the robins warble,
"The summer time" is here,
The month of blushing roses,
The darling of the year.

Wake up, you lazy dreamers!
The summer's waiting you,
The days are long and golden;
The skies are tender blue.

The earth is full of gladness,
Of light and song and bloom,
Join in the summer brightness,
Nor ever think of gloom.

Make haste, June-days to welcome,
For summer-time will fleet
As swift as flying shadows
Across the ripened wheat.

And, when the autumn breezes
Sigh through September's leaves,
And all the sloping hillsides
Wave rows to tasselled sheaves.

The birds that follow summer
Will seek a southern sky,
The sweetness of her blossoms
Will, all forgotten, die.

And summer to her lover
Will yield her weary charms,
Sink peacefully to slumber,
And die in autumn's arms.

Come, then, ye lazy dreamers,
 Come forth to light and love,
The earth is wreathed with garlands,
 The skies are blue above.

The birds their love songs carol
 'Mid golden summer blooms;
The breezes whisper softly
 In twilight's opal glooms;

All glad things bid you welcome
 While last the summer hours.
Who wishes more than June-time,
 With song and light and flowers.

At The Long Sault

("Searching the pile of corpses the victors found four Frenchmen still breathing. Three had scarcely a spark of life . . . the fourth seemed likely to survive and they reserved him for future torments." Parkman's History)

A prisoner under the stars I lie,
With no friend near;
To-morrow they lead me forth to die,
The stake is ready, the torments set,
They will pay in full their deadly debt;
But I fear them not! Oh, none could fear
Of those who stood by Daulac's side —
While he prayed and laughed and sang and fought
In the very reek of death — and caught
The martyr passion that flamed from his face
As he died!

Where he led us we followed glad,
For we loved him well;
Some there were that held him mad,
But we knew that a heavenly rage had place
In that dauntless soul; the good God spake
To us through him; we had naught to do
Save only obey; and when his eyes
Flashed and kindled like storm-swept skies,
And his voice like a trumpet thrilled us through,
We would have marched with delight for his sake
To the jaws of hell.

The mists hung blue and still on the stream
At the marge of dawn;
The rapids laughed till we saw their teeth
Like a snarling wolf's fangs glisten and gleam;
Sweetly the pine trees underneath
The shadows slept in the moonlight wan;
Sweetly beneath the steps of the spring
The great grim forest was blossoming;
And we fought, that springs for other men
Might blossom again.

Faint, thirst-maddened we prayed and fought
By night and by day;
Eyes glared at us with serpent hate —
Yet sometimes a hush fell, and then we heard naught
Save the wind's shrill harping far away,
The piping of birds, and the softened calls
Of the merry distant water-falls;
Then of other scenes we thought —

Of valleys beloved in sunny France,
Purple vineyards of song and dance,
Hopes and visions roseate;
Of many a holy festal morn,
And many a dream at vesper bell —
But anon the shuddering air was torn
By noises such as the fiends of hell
Might make in holding high holiday!
Once, so bitter the death-storm hailed,
We shrank and quailed.

Daulac sprang out before us then,
Shamed in our fears;
Glorious was his face to see,
The face of one who listens and hears
Voices unearthly, summonings high —
Rang his tone like a clarion, "Men,
See yonder star in the golden sky,
Such a man's duty is to him,
A beacon that will not flicker nor dim,
Shining through darkness and despair.
Almost the martyr's crown is yours!
Thinking the price too high to be paid,
Will you leave the sacrifice half made?
I tell you God will answer the prayer
Of the soul that endures!

"Comrades, far in the future I see
A mighty land;
Throned among the nations of earth,
Noble and happy, calm and free;
As a veil were lifted I see her stand,
And out of that future a voice to me
Promises that our names shall shine
On the page of her story with lustre divine
Impelling to visions and deeds of worth.

"Ever thus since the world was begun,
When a man hath given up his life,
Safety and freedom have been won
By the holy power of self-sacrifice;
For the memory of your mother's kiss
Valiantly stand to the breach again.
Comrades, blench not now from the strife,
Quit you like men!"

Oh, we rushed to meet at our captain's side
Death as a bride!
All our brave striplings bravely fell.
I, less fortunate, slowly came
Back from the din of shot and yell
Slowly and gaspingly, to know
A harder fate reserved for me
Than that brief, splendid agony.

Through many a bitter pang and throe
My spirit must to-morrow go
To seek my comrades; but I bear
The tidings that our desperate stand
By the Long Sault has saved our land,
And God has answered Daulac's prayer.

The Prisoner

I lash and writhe against my prison bars,
  And watch with sullen eyes the gaping crowd . . .
Give me my freedom and the burning stars,
  The hollow sky, and crags of moonlit cloud!

Once I might range across the trackless plain,
  And roar with joy, until the desert air
And wide horizons echoed it amain:
  I feared no foe, for I was monarch there!

I saw my shadow on the parching sand,
  When the hot sun had kissed the mountain's rim;
And when the moon rose o'er long wastes of land,
  I sought my prey by some still river's brim;

And with me my fierce love, my tawny mate,
  Meet mother of strong cubs, meet lion's bride . . .
We made our lair in regions desolate,
  The solitude of wildernesses wide.

They slew her . . . and I watched the life-blood flow
  From her torn flank, and her proud eyes grow dim:
I howled her dirge above her while the low,
  Red moon clomb up the black horizon's rim.

Me, they entrapped . . . cowards! They did not dare
  To fight, as brave men do, without disguise,
And face my unleashed rage! The hidden snare
  Was their device to win an untamed prize.

I am a captive . . . not for me the vast,
  White dome of sky above the blinding sand,
The sweeping rapture of the desert blast
  Across long ranges of untrodden land!

Yet still they fetter not my thought . . . in dreams
I, desert-born, tread the hot wastes once more,
Quench my deep thirst in cool, untainted streams,
And shake the darkness with my kingly roar!

The Watchman

"And for fear of Him the keepers did shake, and became as
dead men." — Matthew 28,4.

My Claudia, it is so long since we have met,
So kissed, so held each other heart to heart!
I thought to greet thee as a conqueror comes,
Bearing the trophies of his prowess home,
But Jove hath willed it should be otherwise —
Jove, say I? Nay, some mightier stranger-god
Who thus hath laid his heavy hand on me,
No victor, Claudia, but a broken man
Who seeks to hide his weakness in thy love.

How beautiful thou art! The years have brought
An added splendor to thy loveliness,
With passion of dark eye and lip rose-red
Struggling between its dimple and its pride.
And yet there is somewhat that glooms between
Thy love and mine; come, girdle me about
With thy true arms, and pillow on thy breast
This aching and bewildered head of mine;
Here, where the fountain glitters in the sun
Among the saffron lilies, I will tell —
The shameful fate that hath befallen me.

Down in Jerusalem they slew a man,
Or god — it may be that he was a god . . .
'Twas certain he was poor and meanly born,
No warrior he, nor hero; and he taught
Doctrines that surely would upset the world;
And so they killed him to be rid of him —
Wise, very wise, if he were only man,
Not quite so wise if he were half a god!

I know that strange things happened when he died —
There was a darkness and an agony,
And some were vastly frightened — not so I! . . .
At least he died; and some few friends of his —
I think he had not very many friends —
Took him and laid him in a garden tomb.
A watch was set about the sepulchre,
Lest these, his friends, should hide him and proclaim
That he had risen as he had fore-told.
Laugh not, my Claudia. I laughed when I heard
The prophecy. I would I had not laughed!

I, Maximus, was chosen for the guard
With all my trusty fellows. Pilate knew
I was a man who had no foolish heart
Of softness all unworthy of a man!
My eyes had looked upon a tortured slave
As on a beetle crushed beneath my tread;
I gloried in the splendid strife of war,
Lusting for conquest; I had won the praise
Of our stern general on a scarlet field;
Red in my veins the warrior passion ran,
For I had sprung from heroes, Roman born!

That second night we watched before the tomb;
My men were merry; on the velvet turf,
Bestarred with early blossoms of the Spring,
They diced with jest and laughter; all around
The moonlight washed us like a silver lake,
Save where that silent, sealéd sepulchre

Was hung with shadow as a purple pall.
A faint wind stirred among the olive boughs —
Methinks I hear the sighing of that wind
In all sounds since, it was so dumbly sad;
But as the night wore on it died away
And all was deadly stillness; Claudia,
That stillness was most awful, as if some
Great heart had broken and so ceased to beat!
I thought of many things, but found no joy
In any thought, even the thought of thee;
The moon waned in the west and sickly grew
Her light sucked from her in the breaking dawn —
Never was dawn so welcome as that pale,
Faint glimmer in the cloudless, brooding sky!

Claudia, how may I tell what came to pass?
I have been mocked at when I told the tale
For a crazed dreamer punished by the gods
Because he slept on guard; but mock not *thou!*
I could not bear it if *thy* lips should mock
The vision dread of that Judean morn.

Sudden the pallid east was all aflame
With radiance that beat upon our eyes
As from the noonday sun; and then we saw
Two shapes that were as the immortal gods
Standing before the tomb; around me fell
My men as dead; but I, though through my veins
Ran a cold tremor never known before,
Withstood the shock and saw one shining shape
Roll back the stone; the whole world seemed ablaze,
And through the garden came a rushing wind
Thundering a paeon as of victory.

Then that dead man came forth! Oh, Claudia,
If thou could'st but have seen the face of him!
Never was such a conqueror! Yet no pride
Was in it — nought but love and tenderness,
Such as we Romans scoff at; and his eyes
Bespake him royal . . .

Then he looked full upon me. I had borne
Much staunchly, but that look I could not bear!
What man may front a god and live? I fell
Prone, as if stricken by a thunderbolt;
And, though I died not, somewhat of me died
That made me man. When my long stupor passed
I was no longer Maximus — I was
A weakling with a piteous woman-soul,
All strength and pride, joy and ambition gone —
My Claudia, dare I tell thee what foul curse
Is mine because I looked upon a god?

I care no more for glory; all desire
For conquest and for strife is gone from me,
All eagerness for war; I only care
To help and heal bruised beings, and to give
Some comfort to the weak and suffering . . .

I feel a strange compassion; and I love
All creatures, to the vilest of the slaves
Who seem to me as brothers! Claudia,
Scorn me not for this weakness; it will pass —
Surely 'twill pass in time and I shall be
Maximus strong and valiant once again,
Forgetting that slain god! and yet — and yet —
He looked as one who could not be forgot!

I Feel (Vers Libre)

I feel
Very much
Like taking
Its unholy perpetrators
By the hair
Of their heads
(If they have any hair)
And dragging them around
A few times,
And then cutting them
Into small, irregular pieces
And burying them
In the depths of the blue sea.
They are without form
And void,/ Or at least
The stuff they/ produce
Is./ They are too lazy
To hunt up rhymes;
And that
Is all
That is the matter with them.

The Poet's Thought

It came to him in rainbow dreams,
  Blent with the wisdom of the sages,
  Of spirit and of passion born;
  In words as lucent as the morn
He prisoned it, and now it gleams,
  A jewel shining through the ages.